TEACHER RECOMMENDED

Kids SUMMER ACADEMY

ARGOPREP

7 DAYS A WEEK
8 WEEKS

- Mathematics
- English
- Science
- Reading
- Writing
- Experiments
- Mazes
- Puzzles
- Fitness

GRADE 4-5

ArgoPrep is one of the leading providers of supplemental educational products and services. We offer affordable and effective test prep solutions to educators, parents and students. Learning should be fun and easy! To access more resources visit us at www.argoprep.com.

Our goal is to make your life easier, so let us know how we can help you by e-mailing us at: info@argoprep.com.

- ArgoPrep is a recipient of the prestigious **Mom's Choice Award**.
- ArgoPrep also received the 2019 **Seal of Approval** from Homeschool.com for our award-winning workbooks.
- ArgoPrep was awarded the 2019 **National Parenting Products Award, Gold Medal Parent's Choice Award** and **the Tillywig Brain Child Award.**

ISBN: 978-1946755711
Published by Argo Brothers.

HOW TO USE THE BOOK

Welcome to **Kids Summer Academy** by ArgoPrep.

This workbook is designed to prepare students over the summer to get ready for **Grade 5.** The curriculum has been divided into **eight weeks** so students can complete this entire workbook over the summer.

Our workbook has been carefully designed and **crafted by licensed teachers** to give students an incredible learning experience.

Students start off the week with English activities followed by Math practice. Throughout the week, students have several fitness activities to complete. Making sure students stay active is just as important as practicing mathematics.

We introduce yoga and other basic fitness activities that any student can complete. Each week includes a science experiment which sparks creativity and allows students to visually understand the concepts. On the last day of each week, students will work on a fun puzzle.

HOW TO WATCH VIDEO EXPLANATIONS

IT IS ABSOLUTELY FREE

Go to **argoprep.com/summer5**
OR scan the QR Code:

TABLE OF CONTENTS

TABLE OF CONTENTS

TABLE OF CONTENTS

Completed your summer journey?

Craving more insights? Follow the link provided or simply scan the QR code to access exclusive **BONUS** materials!

argoprep.com/summer5

KIDS SUMMER ACADEMY SERIES

ArgoPrep's **Kids Summer Academy** series helps prevent summer learning loss and gets students ready for their new school year by reinforcing core foundations in math, english and science. Our workbooks also introduce new concepts so students can get a head start and be on top of their game for the new school year!

WATER FIRE
GREEN DRAGON WARRIOR
THUNDER WARRIOR
MYSTICAL NINJA
GREEN POISON
ADRASTOS THE SUPER WARRIOR
CAPTAIN ARGO
FIRESTORM WARRIOR
DANCE HERO
CAPTAIN BRAVERY
RAPID NINJA
Give your character a name
Write down the special ability or powers your character has and how you will help your community with the powers.
Great! You are all set. To become an incredible hero, we need to strengthen our skills in **English, math,** and **science**. Let's get started.

Welcome!
We will begin our journey on
Mercury, one of the eight planets
in our solar system.
WEEK 1
Mercury is the smallest planet
in our Solar System.
Did you know one year on Mercury is just
88 days long!

WEEK 1 DAY 1

OVERVIEW OF ENGLISH CONCEPTS
SYNONYMS & ANTONYMS

As you continue to grow as a reader and a writer, it's important to keep developing your vocabulary. To be an effective communicator, you must know as many ways to articulate your ideas as possible. As a reader and listener, you need to be able to figure out what people are saying! One great vocabulary builder is to study **synonyms** and **antonyms.** **Synonyms** are words that work similarly in a sentence and have the **same** meaning. **Antonyms** are words that have completely **opposite** meanings.

Key Terms

Synonyms: Words that have the same meaning

Antonyms: Words that have opposite meanings

For Example...

Example Word	Synonyms	Antonyms
Big	Huge, Gigantic, Large, Sizable, Massive, Colossal, Titanic, Gargantuan, etc.	Small, Little, Tiny, Miniature, Minute, Modest, Minuscule, etc.
Smart	Intelligent, Brilliant, Clever, Bright, Cerebral, Sharp-witted, savvy, etc.	Dumb, Stupid, Unintelligent, Ignorant, Foolish, Dense, Idiotic, Ignorant, etc.
New	Modern, Recent, State-of-the-Art, Cutting-Edge, Current, Up-to-Date, etc.	Old, Existing, Antique, Hackneyed, Tired, Stale, Staid, etc.
Simple	Easy, Straightforward, Uncomplicated, Effortless, Painless, Elementary, etc.	Difficult, Tough, Hard, Strenuous Complex, Demanding, Grueling, Exhausting, Back-Breaking, etc.
Hot	Warm, Balmy, Roasting, Scorching, Blistering, Sweltering, etc.	Cold, Chilly, Tepid, Arctic, Freezing, Frosty, Cool, Wintry, etc.

When you write, instead of repeating the same basic words over and over again, spice up your descriptions by using synonyms and antonyms.

From "Japanese Fairy Tales"

By Yea Theodora Ozaki

Not long ago in China, there was a wonderful invention called the shinansha. This was a kind of chariot with the figure of a man on it always pointing to the South. No matter how the chariot was placed the figure always wheeled about and pointed to the South.

This curious instrument was invented by Kotei, one of the three Chinese Emperors of the Mythological age. Kotei was the son of the Emperor Yuhi. Before he was born his mother had a vision which foretold that her son would be a great man.

One summer evening she went out to walk in the meadows to seek the cool breezes which blow at the end of the day and to gaze with pleasure at the star-lit heavens above her. As she looked at the North Star, strange to relate, it shot forth vivid flashes of lightning in every direction. Soon after this her son Kotei came into the world.

Kotei in time grew to manhood and succeeded his father the Emperor Yuhi. His early reign was greatly troubled by the rebel Shiyu. This rebel wanted to make himself King, and many were the battles which he fought to this end. Shiyu was a wicked magician, his head was made of iron, and there was no man that could conquer him.

At last Kotei declared war against the rebel and led his army to battle, and the two armies met on a plain called Takuroku. The Emperor boldly attacked the enemy, but the magician brought down a dense fog upon the battlefield, and while the royal army were wandering about in confusion, trying to find their way, Shiyu retreated with his troops, laughing at having fooled the royal army.

No matter however strong and brave the Emperor's soldiers were, the rebel with his magic could always escape in the end.

1. What do you think the author means when she says Shiyu's "head was made of iron"?

____

____

2. What are two different ways the author foreshadows or suggests that Kotei will grow up to be a very important person before the character is even born in the story?

____

____

____

____

3. Which of these words is an **antonym** for "rebel" as it is used in Paragraph 4?

   A. Fighter
   B. Ally
   C. Ungrateful
   D. Peace

4. Which of these words is a **synonym** for "retreated" as it is used in Paragraph 5?

   A. Attacked
   B. Reinvented
   C. Withdrew
   D. Used magic

5. How do you predict the "shinansha" you read about at the beginning of the passage might be involved in the resolution of the story?

____

____

____

____

____

____

Identifying Synonyms

Directions:

Read each sentence and make sure to think about how the underlined word is being used. Then, circle the word from the pair in parentheses after the sentence that is a **synonym** for the underlined word in the sentence.

1. I was so upset when I didn't win the tennis tournament that I couldn't focus on how great an accomplishment it was to finish second until years afterward. (FRUSTRATED / SURPRISED)

2. The power went out in our neighborhood because a delivery truck skidded on ice and knocked down the power lines. (TOWN / COMMUNITY)

3. Although electric and acoustic guitars are quite similar, there are very different techniques for playing them. (QUALITIES / STRATEGIES)

4. At least five players scrambled to recover the loose basketball, but Alicia got to it first. (RUSHED / MIXED UP)

5. Miguel and Chloe have been the strongest math students in our class since kindergarten. (BIGGEST / MOST CAPABLE)

FITNESS

Please be aware of your environment and be safe at all times. If you cannot do an exercise, just try your best.

Repeat these exercises **3 ROUNDS**

1 - Abs: 10 times

2 - Lunges: 5 times to each leg.
Note: Use your body weight or books as weight to do leg lunges.

3 - Plank: 15 sec.

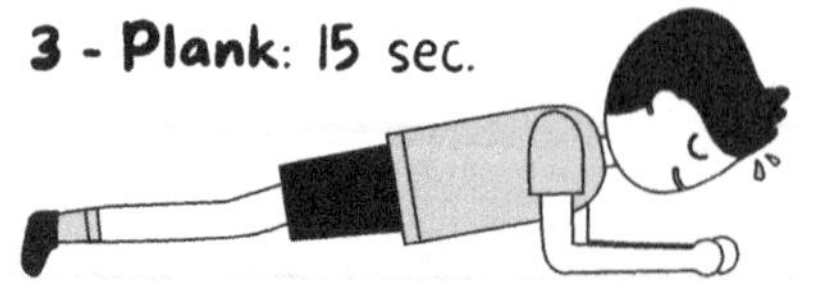

4 - Run: 50m
Note: Run 25 meters to one side and 25 meters back to the starting position.

From "Japanese Fairy Tales"

By Yea Theodora Ozaki

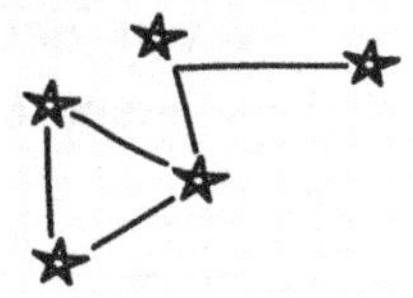

(Continued from Day 1's Passage)

Kotei returned to his Palace, and thought and pondered deeply as to how he should conquer the magician, for he was determined not to give up yet. After a long time he invented the shinansha with the figure of a man always pointing South, for there were no compasses in those days. With this instrument to show him the way he need not fear the dense fogs raised up by the magician to confound his men.

Kotei again declared war against Shiyu. He placed the shinansha in front of his army and led the way to the battlefield.

The battle began in earnest. The rebel was being driven backward by the royal troops when he again resorted to magic, and upon his saying some strange words in a loud voice, immediately a dense fog came down upon the battlefield.

But this time no soldier minded the fog, not one was confused. Kotei by pointing to the shinansha could find his way and directed the army without a single mistake. He closely pursued the rebel army and drove them backward till they came to a big river. This river Kotei and his men found was swollen by the floods and impossible to cross.

Shiyu by using his magic art quickly passed over with his army and shut himself up in a fortress on the opposite bank.

When Kotei found his march checked he was wild with disappointment, for he had very nearly overtaken the rebel when the river stopped him.

He could do nothing, for there were no boats in those days, so the Emperor ordered his tent to be pitched in the pleasantest spot that the place afforded.

One day he stepped forth from his tent and after walking about for a short time he came to a pond. Here he sat down on the bank and was lost in thought.

It was autumn. The trees growing along the edge of the water were shedding their leaves, which floated hither and thither on the surface of the pond. By and by, Kotei's attention was attracted to a spider on the brink of the water. The little insect was trying to get on to one of the floating leaves nearby. It did so at last, and was soon floating over the water to the other side of the pond.

This little incident made the clever Emperor think that he might try to make something that could carry himself and his men over the river in the same way that the leaf had carried over the spider.

1. What details from this story help the reader clearly know that they are reading a myth or fairy tale?

2. What idea does Kotei get from the spider at the end of the passage?

3. Which of these words is a **synonym** for "instrument" as it is used in Paragraph 1?

   A. Guitar
   B. Secret
   C. Tool
   D. Instructions

4. Which of these words is an **antonym** for "pleasantest" as it is used in Paragraph 7?

   A. Nicest
   B. Magical
   C. Smoothest
   D. Worst

5. Now that you have read two different passages about Emperor Kotei, describe him in your own words. What kind of a person and leader is he?

WEEK 1 DAY 2

ACTIVITIES
SYNONYMS & ANTONYMS

Identifying Antonyms

Directions:

Read each sentence and make sure to think about how the underlined word is being used. Then, circle the word from the pair in parentheses after the sentence that is an antonym for the underlined word in the sentence.

1. After I was sick with pneumonia, I felt frail for months because I had lost so much weight. (ROBUST / UNHEALTHY)

2. The town of Oak Hills is building a skate park for local kids to enjoy. (FORGET / DREAD)

3. Poison oak and poison ivy both have clustered leaves with three distinct points. (FALLEN / SCATTERED)

4. The dog tugged a sled behind him that contained firewood his owner had gathered from the forest. (RAN / PUSHED)

5. I started to feel dizzy when we were at the top of the lighthouse because I don't deal well with heights. (POORLY / GOOD)

FITNESS

Please be aware of your environment and be safe at all times. If you cannot do an exercise, just try your best.

Repeat these exercises **3 ROUNDS**

1 - Squats: 15 times. Note: imagine you are trying to sit on a chair.

2 - Side Bending: 10 times to each side. Note: try to touch your feet.

3 - Tree Pose: Stay as long as possible. Note: do the same with the other leg.

Addition Practice Questions

1. Which pair of numbers have a sum of 7,635?

A. 2,467 and 5,168
B. 3,745 and 3,980
C. 5,243 and 1,862
D. 4,168 and 3,257

2. Which of the following number sentences is true?

A. 3,478 + 2,385 = 5,763
B. 6,712 + 4,532 = 11,234
C. 3,493 + 1,275 = 4,768
D. 3,976 + 6,534 = 10,410

3. What is the sum of 2,479 and 1,365?

A. 3,834
B. 3,844
C. 3,854
D. 3,864

4. What is 56,878 + 23,134?

A. 79,812
B. 79,912
C. 80,002
D. 80,012

5. Which number should be added to 4,863 to get the number 13,184?

A. 8,131
B. 8,321
C. 8,361
D. 8,451

6. What is 25,738 + 14,627? Write your answer below.

____

7. Write and solve an addition sentence using these two numbers:

36,753 and 6,842

____

8. What is 4,736 + 2,389 + 3,628?

Answer ______________________

9. Which of the following number sentences is FALSE?

A. 2,700 + 134 = 2,600 + 234
B. 4,532 + 1,739 = 1,739 + 4,532
C. 6,834 + 3,627 = 3,517 + 6,734
D. 32,943 + 25,765 = 24,765 + 33,943

10. Fill in the blank to make an equal problem.

2,165 + _________ + 1,678 = 6,414

Subtraction Practice Questions

1. What is 2,376 - 1,385?

A. 961
B. 991
C. 1,011
D. 1,121

2. Which answer choice results 2,194?

A. 8,849 - 6,575
B. 3,472 - 1,188
C. 7,347 - 4,952
D. 6,572 - 4,378

WEEK 1 DAY 3  MATH

3. What is the difference between 2,765 and 4,383?

   A. 1,618
   B. 1,628
   C. 1,698
   D. 1,738

4. What is the missing number in the equation 5,174 - _______ = 1,998?

   A. 2,956
   B. 3,116
   C. 3,176
   D. 3,226

5. Which expression is true?

   A. 2,367 - 1,145 = 1222
   B. 6738 - 3,862 = 2776
   C. 4382 - 2,874 = 1518
   D. 7245 - 6,581 = 674

6. What is the missing number in the equation below?
   4,729 - ________ = 1,241

7. What is the difference between 27,399 and 34,826?

   Answer ____________________

8. Use subtraction to solve the following problem.

```
  3,758
- 2,735
```

   Answer ____________________

9. Look at this expression
   68,371 - 54,729 = 13,562. Is it true?
   If not, write the correct answer.

   ____

10. Use subtraction to solve the following problem.

```
  6,839
- 3,726
```

   Answer ____________________

FITNESS ☆

Please be aware of your environment and be safe at all times. If you cannot do an exercise, just try your best.

Repeat these exercises **3 ROUNDS**

1 - Bend forward: 10 times.
Note: try to touch your feet. Make sure to keep your back straight and if needed you can bend your knees.

2 - Lunges: 5 times to each leg.
Note: Use your body weight or books as weight to do leg lunges.

3 - Plank: 15 sec.

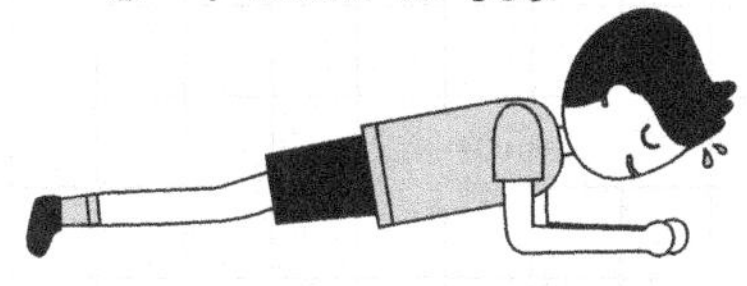

4 - Abs: 10 times

Multiplication Practice Questions

1. Find the product of 56 and 39.

   A. 1,894
   B. 2,184
   C. 2,374
   D. 2,894

2. Choose the pair of numbers that results in a product of 2,001.

   A. 47 and 33
   B. 59 and 49
   C. 17 and 43
   D. 23 and 87

3. You can get the number 26,376 by multiplying 7 by the number____.

   A. 3,768
   B. 2,958
   C. 3,498
   D. 4,018

4. Which expression can be used to find 280 times 46?

   A. 28 x 46 + 10 x 46
   B. (28 + 10) x 46
   C. 28 x 46 x 10
   D. 28 x (46 + 10)

5. What is the missing number in the equation _______ x 6 = 35,364?

   A. 4,874
   B. 5,894
   C. 5,984
   D. 6,134

6. Choose the right multiplier for 28 to get 1,092.

   A. 34
   B. 39
   C. 44
   D. 48

7. What is (37 x 42) + (78 x 25)?

   Answer ______________________

8. Write the expression 164 + 164 + 164 + 164 + 164 + 164 +164 using multiplication.

   ____

9. Determine the number that correctly fills in the blank.

   180 x ________ = 720

10. Solve the problem 340 x 68.

    Answer ______________________

Division Practice Questions

1. Find the divider of 3,918 to get 653.

   A. 4
   B. 5
   C. 6
   D. 7

2. Which number sentence below is true?

   A. 356 ÷ 4 = 300 + 56 ÷ 4
   B. (674 + 30 + 6) ÷ 4 = 710 ÷ 4
   C. 200 ÷ 5 + 400 ÷ 5 = 600 ÷ 5
   D. 458 ÷ 6 = 400 ÷ (6 + 58) ÷ 6

WEEK 1 DAY 4  MATH

3. How many times is the number 7 less than the number 3,948?

   A. 474
   B. 494
   C. 534
   D. 564

4. What is the quotient when 3,658 is divided by 9?

   A. 399 r 8
   B. 406 r 4
   C. 412 r 7
   D. 431 r 2

5. What is 1,359 ÷ 3?

   A. 453
   B. 473
   C. 493
   D. 513

6. What is (6,000 + 111) ÷ 7 = ?

   Answer ______________________

7. The perimeter of an equilateral triangle is 1,407 in. What is the length of one side?

   Answer ______________________

8. What is the missing number in the equation?

   4,664 ÷ _______ = 8

9. Determine the number that correctly fills in the blank.

   675 ÷ _______ = 75

10. Use multiplication rules to determine the missing remainder for the problem.

    748 ÷ 5 = 149 r _____

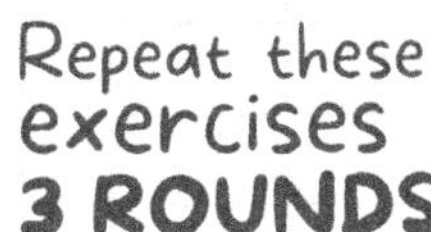

FITNESS

☆ Please be aware of your environment and be safe at all times. If you cannot do an exercise, just try your best.

Repeat these exercises **3 ROUNDS**

2 - Chair: 20 sec.
Note: sit on an imaginary chair, keep your back straight.

1 - High Plank: 15 sec.

3 - Waist Hooping: 20 times. Note: if you do not have a hoop, pretend you have an imaginary hoop and rotate your hips 20 times.

4 - Abs: 10 times

WEEK 1 DAY 5  MATH

Word problems of add/subtract/multiply/divide

1. Mrs. Peterson bought 300 candies at the store, and then she came back to buy 5 times more for her family of 4. How many candies will each member of her family get if the candies are divided equally?

   A. 350
   B. 400
   C. 450
   D. 490

2. Iren drew stars on a sheet of scrap paper. She drew 16 stars on the front and seven stars on the back. How many stars did she draw in total if she used 13 sheets to draw the same number of stars?

   A. 247
   B. 299
   C. 341
   D. 358

3. Mr. Davis bought 1,267 nails for repairs. If he only used 835, how many nails does he have left?

   A. 432
   B. 482
   C. 392
   D. 512

4. Avery writes 765 words a day. Madison writes 2,295 a day. How many times more words does Madison write than Avery?

   Answer ____________________

5. Jacob earned $ 1,341 cleaning cars over the summer. If he only had 9 customers and each person paid the same amount, how much did each person pay?

   A. 138
   B. 145
   C. 149
   D. 153

6. A store sold 14 times more cartons of milk than packs of butter. If they sold 280 cartons of milk, how many packs of butter did they sell?

   Answer ____________________

7. Ian loves to draw. Each day he draws 48 pictures. How many pictures will he have drawn after 25 days?

   Answer ____________________

8. Ann used fourteen colorful pencils to draw pictures. Her friend Liz used 5 times as many as Ann. How many pencils did they use in total?

   Answer ____________________

9. In school a math book costs 6 times as much as a history book. If the history book costs three dollars, how much would 26 math books cost?

   Answer ____________________

10. Max was collecting paper for recycling. In 6 months he had collected 75 boxes with 8 kilograms of paper inside each box.

    How many kilograms of paper did he have in total?

    Answer ____________________

WEEK 1 DAY 5  MATH

Diagrams: add/subtract/multiply/divide

1. Use the model below to solve the problem 3,245 + 2,428.

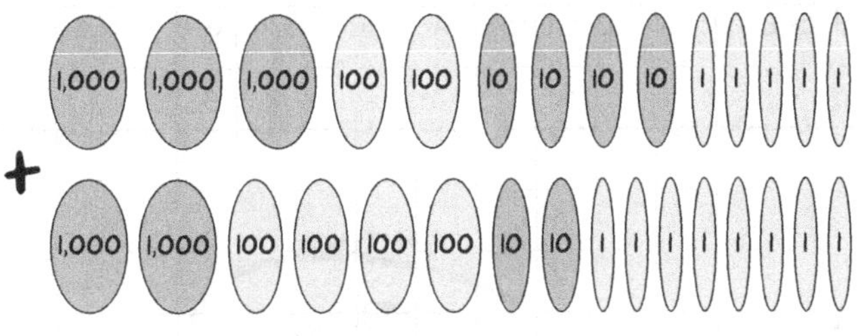

A. 5,468
B. 5,575
C. 5,668
D. 5,673

2. Which equation does the number line most likely represent?

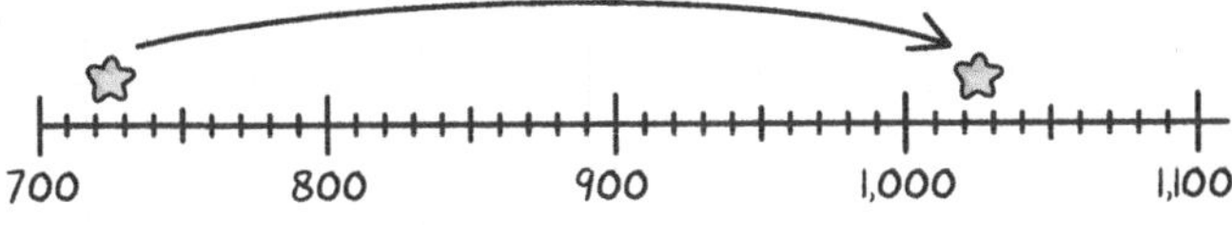

A. 725 + 298 = 1,023
B. 730 + 350 = 1,080
C. 750 + 350 = 1,100
D. 700 + 400 = 1,100

3. Use the model to solve the multiplication problem 2,350 x 5.

Answer ______________________

4. Nine squirrels ate an equal number of acorns over a certain period of time. They ate 2,880 in total. How many acorns did each squirrel eat? One ◎ represents 10.

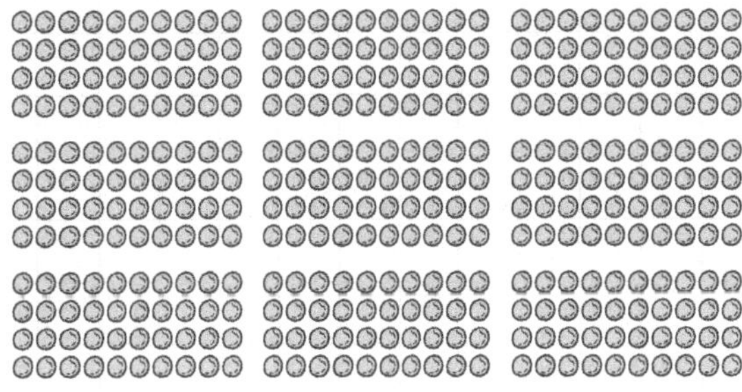

Answer ______________________

5. Solve 720 ÷ 6. Use 🛸 as 10.

Answer ______________________

YOGA

Please be aware of your environment and be safe at all times. If you cannot do an exercise, just try your best.

1 - Down Dog: 20 sec.

2 - Bend Down: 20 sec.

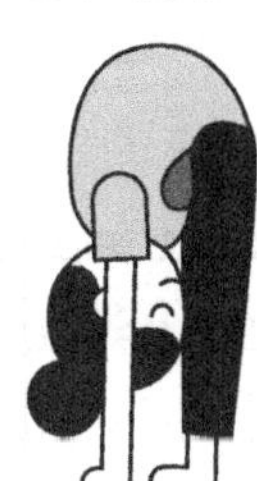

3 - Chair: 20 sec.

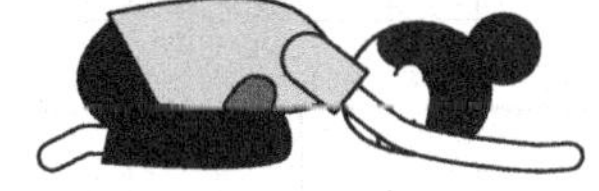

4 - Child Pose: 20 sec.

5 - Shavasana: as long as you can. Note: think of happy moments and relax your mind.

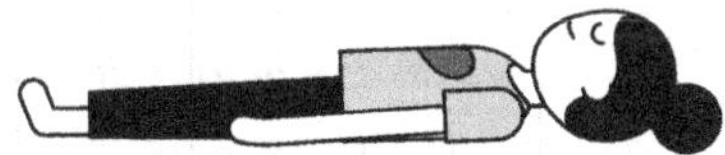

WEEK 1 DAY 6 SCIENCE EXPERIMENT

Identifying Basic Elements

Everything in the universe is made of **matter**. That means that everything has a **mass** and **takes up space**. No matter how tiny or microscopic something is, it still has a **mass** and is made of **matter**. Matter is made up of tiny particles known as **atoms**. **Atoms** represent the pure building-block form of the **elements**. Today, we'll create some atoms and learn about a few of the most basic elements.

Materials:

- 2 different sizes of Styrofoam balls
  - **6** small Styrofoam balls
  - **5** medium-sized Styrofoam balls
- 3 different color markers
- An encyclopedia or internet access for research
- Note paper

Procedure:

1. Take the **6** small Styrofoam balls and, using one of your markers, draw a big "H" on both sides of each one. These balls represent **Hydrogen** atoms for our experiments.
2. Take **3** of the medium-sized Styrofoam balls and, using a different color marker, draw a big "O" on both sides of each one. These balls represent **Oxygen** atoms for our experiments.
3. Take the remaining **2** medium-sized balls and, using your third different color of marker, draw a big "C" on both sides of each one. These balls represent **Carbon** atoms for our experiments.
4. Using your encyclopedia or internet research tools, look up **Hydrogen** and write five important facts about hydrogen in your notes.
5. Using your encyclopedia or internet research tools, look up **Oxygen** and write five important facts about oxygen in your notes.
6. Using your encyclopedia or internet research tools, look up **Carbon** and write five important facts about carbon in your notes.
7. After you've created your atoms and researched the three elements we are focusing on, store your notes and atoms in a safe place so we can use them in our next science activity.

WEEK 1 DAY 6 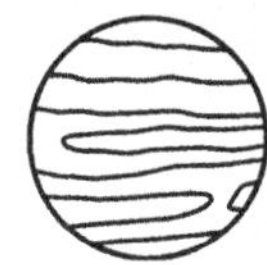 EXPERIMENT

Follow-Up Questions:

1. Based on your research, what is a common characteristic or trait between Hydrogen, Carbon, and Oxygen?

2. Why do you think we are using different sized Styrofoam balls to represent different elements? What do you predict that represents?

YOGA

Please be aware of your environment and be safe at all times. If you cannot do an exercise, just try your best.

3 - Stretching: Stay as long as possible.
Note: do on one leg then on another.

4 - Lower Plank: 20 sec.
Note: Keep your back straight and body tight.

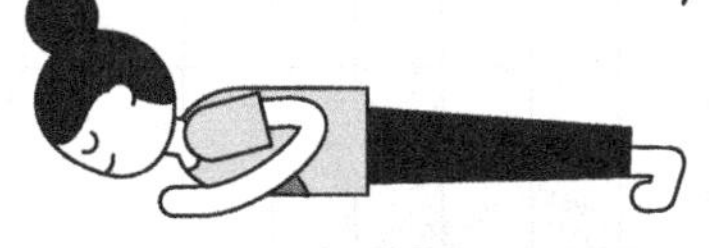

2 - Down Dog: 20 sec.

1 - Tree Pose: Stay as long as possible.
Note: do on one leg then on another.

START

6 - Shavasana: 10 min.
Note: this pose is very important and provides you with long term benefits. Try not to skip this. Close your eyes and imagine who you want to be and what your goals are! Always think happy thoughts.

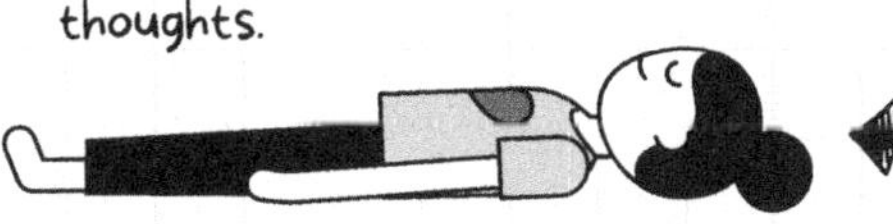

5 - Book Pose: 20 sec.
Note: Keep your core tight. Legs should be across from your eyes.

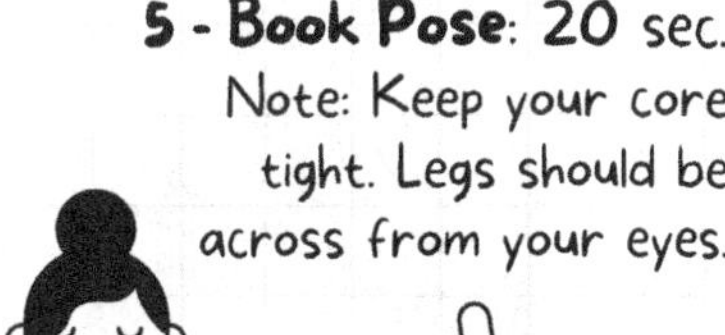

WEEK 1 DAY 7 MAZE

Task: Yikes! After a concert, the guitar cables are all messed up. Help the musicians by connecting the guitar number with the appropriate letter for the amplifier.

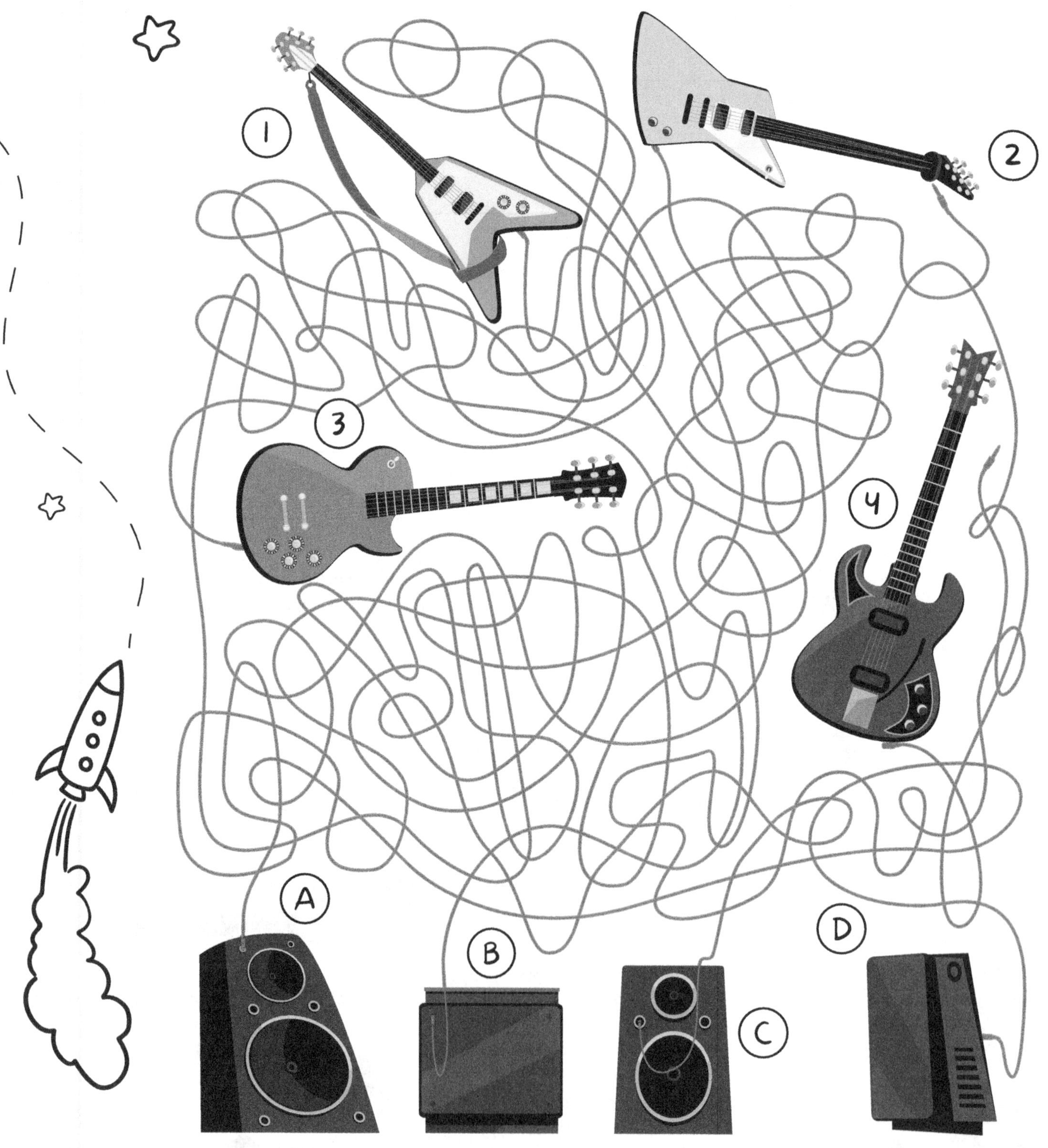

Answers: ______________________

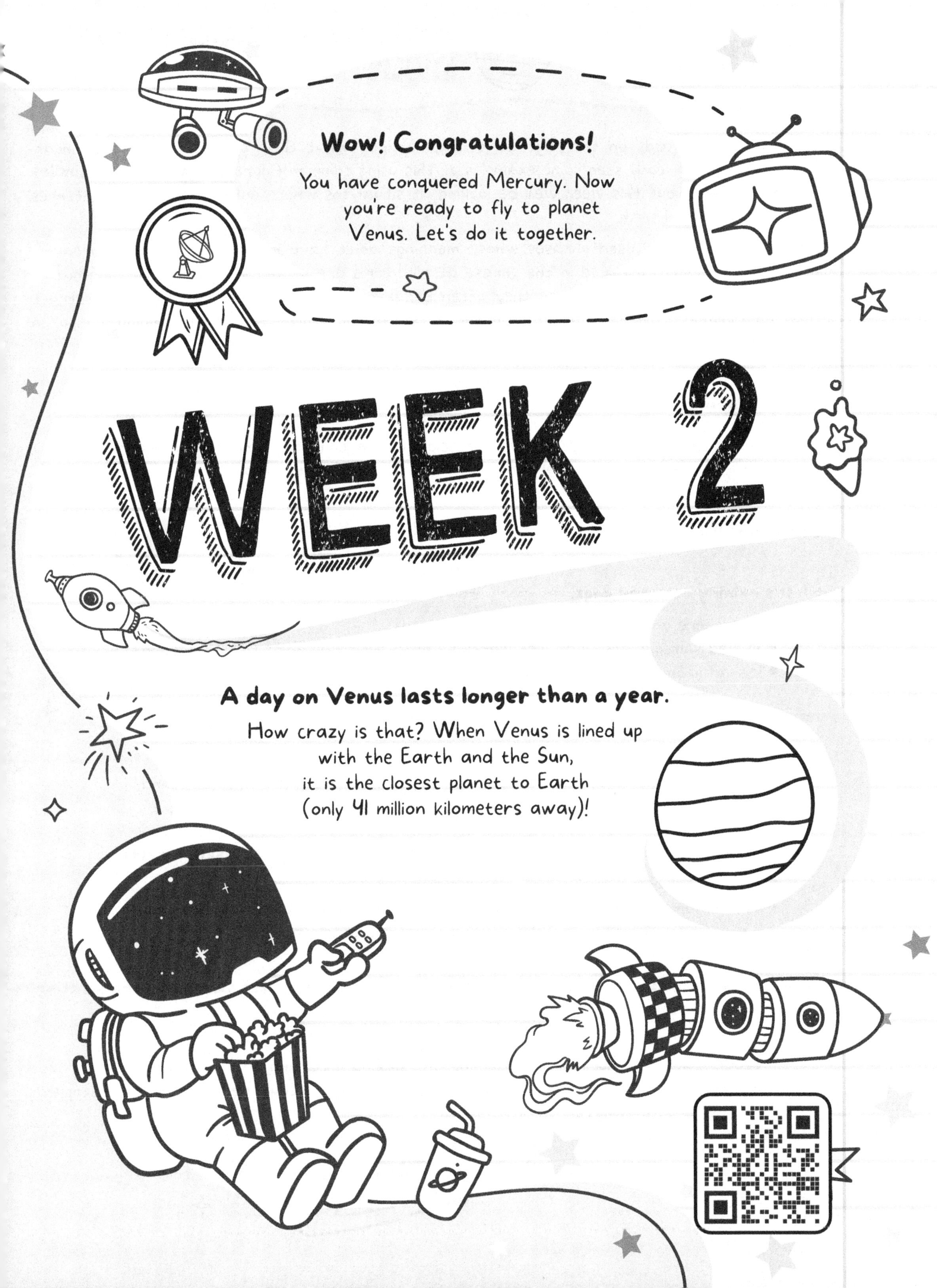

Wow! Congratulations!

You have conquered Mercury. Now you're ready to fly to planet Venus. Let's do it together.

WEEK 2

A day on Venus lasts longer than a year.

How crazy is that? When Venus is lined up with the Earth and the Sun, it is the closest planet to Earth (only 41 million kilometers away)!

WEEK 2 DAY 1  OVERVIEW OF ENGLISH CONCEPTS IDIOMS

Sometimes, the words on the page don't mean exactly what their definitions say they mean. You've probably already seen some examples of this using common figurative language like **similes** and **metaphors**, but this week we'll be looking at situations where entire phrases or sentences are not what they seem.

Idioms are commonly used phrases whose meanings don't have much to do with the meaning of the actual words involved in the phrase at all. Idioms are usually very tough for non-native English speakers to learn because they often break or ignore the ways we usually construct meaning. However, decoding and using idioms is crucial for a high-level understanding of spoken and written English.

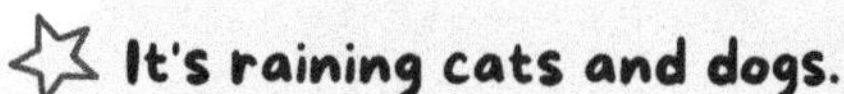

Key Terms

Idiom: A group of words or an expression whose commonly understood meaning is only minimally connected to the literal definitions of the words it contains.

For Example...

It's raining cats and dogs.

- Are there any actual cats or dogs involved?
- Would someone who was just learning English find this hard to understand?
- It's an idiom meaning "It's raining extremely hard!"

I don't want to do my math homework, but I guess I need to bite the bullet.

- Are there any actual bullets involved?
- Would someone who was just learning English find this hard to understand?
- It's an idiom meaning "I just have to do it, even though it's uncomfortable."

After our scary trip through the haunted house, I had to pull myself together.

- Does this process involve any actual pulling?
- Would someone who was just learning English find this hard to understand?
- It's an idiom meaning "To calm down and resume acting normally."

When the middle of my pot pie was still frozen, it was the last straw as far as eating school lunches.

- Does this process involve any actual straws?
- Would someone who was just learning English find this hard to understand?
- It's an idiom meaning "It was the final frustrating thing I could deal with before I stopped putting up with things."

From "Adrift in New York"

By Horatio Alger

"Uncle, you are not looking well to-night."

"I'm not well, Florence. I sometimes doubt if I shall ever be any better."

"Surely, uncle, you cannot mean..."

"Yes, my child, I have reason to believe that I am nearing the end."

"I cannot bear to hear you speak so, uncle," said Florence Linden, in irrepressible agitation. "You are not an old man. You are but fifty-four."

"True, Florence, but it is not years only that make a man old. Two great sorrows have embittered my life. First, the death of my dearly beloved wife, and next, the loss of my boy, Harvey."

"It is long since I have heard you refer to my cousin's loss. I thought you had become reconciled - no, I do not mean that, - I thought your regret might be less poignant."

"I have not permitted myself to speak of it, but I have never ceased to think of it day and night."

John Linden paused sadly, then resumed:

"If he had died, I might, as you say, have become reconciled; but he was abducted at the age of four by a revengeful servant whom I had discharged from my employment. "Heaven knows whether he is living or dead, but it is impressed upon my mind that he still lives, it may be in misery, it may be as a criminal, while I, his unhappy father, live on in luxury which I cannot enjoy, with no one to care for me"

Florence Linden sank impulsively on her knees beside her uncle's chair.

"Don't say that, uncle," she pleaded. "You know that I love you, Uncle John."

1. Based on the passage, how would you describe Florence's personality?

2. Why do you think John Linden decided to tell Florence the real story about his son?

3. Which of these is an example of an **idiom**?

A. "I am nearing the end..." (Paragraph 4)
B. "You are not an old man..." (Paragraph 5)
C. "I thought you had become reconciled..." (Paragraph 7)
D. "I thought your regret might be less poignant..." (Paragraph 7)

4. Which of these is an example of a **proverb** or **adage**?

A. "You are not an old man..." (Paragraph 5)
B. "... the death of my dearly beloved wife" (Paragraph 6)
C. "... it is not years only that make a man old" (Paragraph 6)
D. "Two great sorrows have embittered my life..." (Paragraph 6)

5. Why does John Linden find it more difficult to get over his son being kidnapped rather than killed?

WEEK 2 DAY 1 ACTIVITIES IDIOMS

Identifying and Defining Idioms

Directions:

Read each sentence and underline the idiom contained in each one. On the line below the sentence, explain what the idiom actually means in your own words.

1. Some people say you can't teach an old dog new tricks, but my grandma loves to play video games.

2. Saul told me he was moving to Australia to study kangaroos the other day, but I think he was pulling my leg.

3. That math test that everybody was worried about turned out to be a piece of cake.

4. I am trying to make time to go to the football game this weekend, but I have got a lot on my plate.

5. My dad missed the boat on cell phones, and now he always complains that he doesn't know how to operate his.

FITNESS

Please be aware of your environment and be safe at all times. If you cannot do an exercise, just try your best.

Repeat these exercises **3 ROUNDS**

1 - Abs: 10 times

2 - Lunges: 5 times to each leg.
Note: Use your body weight or books as weight to do leg lunges.

3 - Plank: 15 sec.

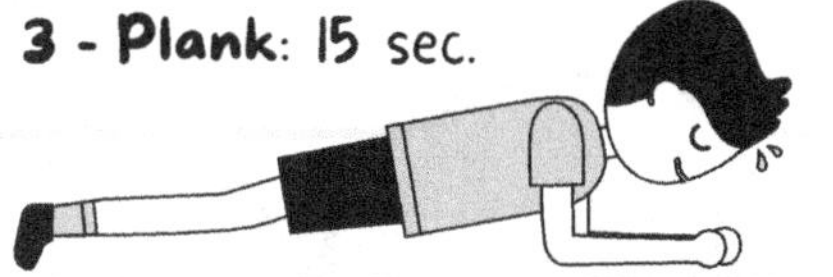

4 - Run: 50m
Note: Run 25 meters to one side and 25 meters back to the starting position.

From "Adrift in New York"

By Horatio Alger

(Continued from Day 1's Passage)

"And I, too, uncle."

There was a shade of jealousy in the voice of Curtis Waring as he entered the library through the open door, and approaching his uncle, pressed his hand.

He was a tall, dark-complexioned man, of perhaps thirty-five, with shifty, black eyes and thin lips, shaded by a dark mustache. It was not a face to trust.

Even when he smiled the expression of his face did not soften. Yet he could moderate his voice so as to express tenderness and sympathy.

He was the son of an elder sister of Mr. Linden, while Florence was the daughter of a younger brother.

Both were orphans, and both formed a part of Mr. Linden's household, and owed everything to his bounty.

Curtis was supposed to be in some business downtown; but he received a liberal allowance from his uncle, and often drew upon him for outside assistance.

As he stood with his uncle's hand in his, he was necessarily brought near Florence, who instinctively drew a little away, with a slight shudder indicating repugnance.

Slight as it was, Curtis detected it, and his face darkened.

John Linden looked from one to the other. "Yes," he said, "I must not forget that I have a nephew and a niece. You are both dear to me, but no one can take the place of the boy I have lost."

1. How are Curtis and Florence different from each other? (You can include details from the Day 1 passage in your answer, as well as details from this passage.)

2. Why does Florence lack love and respect for Curtis?

3. Based on the text, which of these **adages** about money would Curtis probably agree with the most?

A. A penny saved is a penny earned.
B. Money doesn't grow on trees.
C. The best things in life are free.
D. You have to spend money to make money.

4. Based on the text, which of these things do we definitely know about John?

A. He has a strong sense of family
B. He is poor
C. He is very old
D. He has no children of his own

5. What does each character want to achieve or get out of this moment? Why is John telling this story after so many years? What is Curtis trying to prove? What does Florence want?

Proverbs & Adages

Directions:

Proverbs and adages are idioms meant to communicate wisdom in a short, witty way. Read each proverb or adage below, and then, in your own words, explain what the statement means. After which, describe why that viewpoint would be seen as wise or a good idea.(If you have trouble decoding any of these, feel free to use the internet or a reference book to help come up with a definition. Then, use your own words and thoughts to explain why that would be considered wise.)

1. **A penny saved is a penny earned.**

   EXPLANATION ____

   ____

   WHY IS THAT CONSIDERED WISE? ______________________________

   ____

2. **United we stand, divided we fall.**

   EXPLANATION ____

   ____

   WHY IS THAT CONSIDERED WISE? ______________________________

   ____

3. **Things are not always what they seem.**

   EXPLANATION ____

   ____

   WHY IS THAT CONSIDERED WISE? ______________________________

   ____

4. **It's better to be safe than sorry.**

   EXPLANATION ____

   ____

WHY IS THAT CONSIDERED WISE? ____

____

5. **Where there's smoke, there's fire.**

EXPLANATION ____

____

WHY IS THAT CONSIDERED WISE? ____

____

FITNESS

Please be aware of your environment and be safe at all times. If you cannot do an exercise, just try your best.

Repeat these exercises **3 ROUNDS**

1 - Squats: 15 times. Note: imagine you are trying to sit on a chair.

2 - Side Bending: 10 times to each side. Note: try to touch your feet.

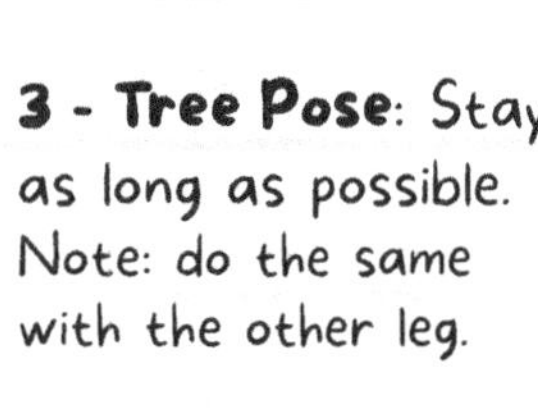

3 - Tree Pose: Stay as long as possible. Note: do the same with the other leg.

4 - High Plank: 15 sec.

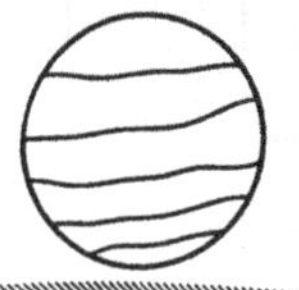

Diagrams: add/subtract/multiply/divide

1. Which expression best represents the model below?

A. 1,268 + 2,346 x 4
B. 4 x 1,268 + 2,346
C. (1,268 + 2,346) x 4
D. (1,268 + 2,346) x 5

2. What is the divisor of 1,184 to get 148?

A. 5
B. 6
C. 7
D. 8

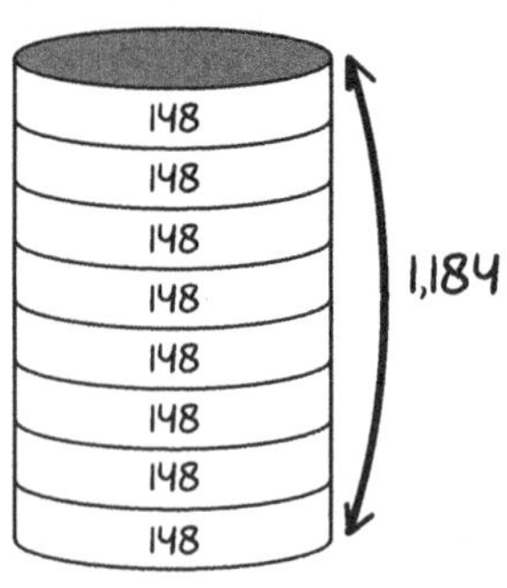

3. Which expression best represents the picture below? = 15.

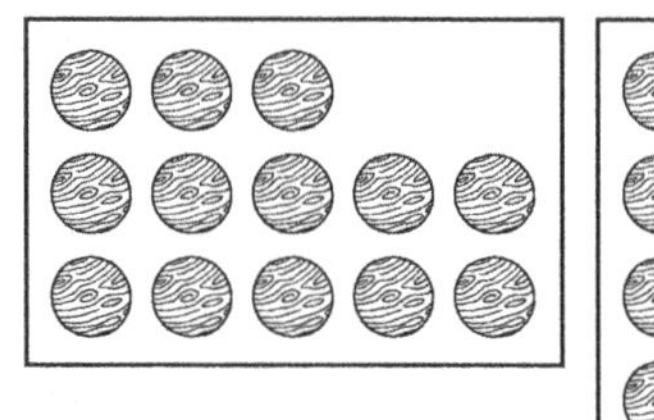

A. 13 + 23 = 26
B. 195 + 345 = 540
C. 65 + 115 = 180
D. 13 + 23 x 15 = 358

4. What is the quotient and remainder in the division problem modeled below?

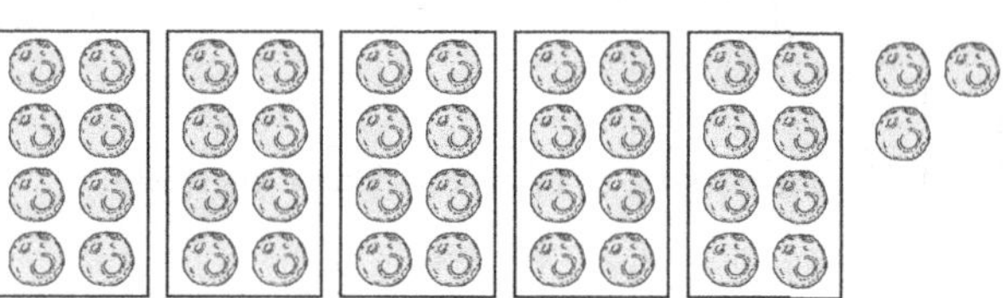

Answer ______________________

5. Use the model below to solve this problem 2,800 - 1,260. = 70.

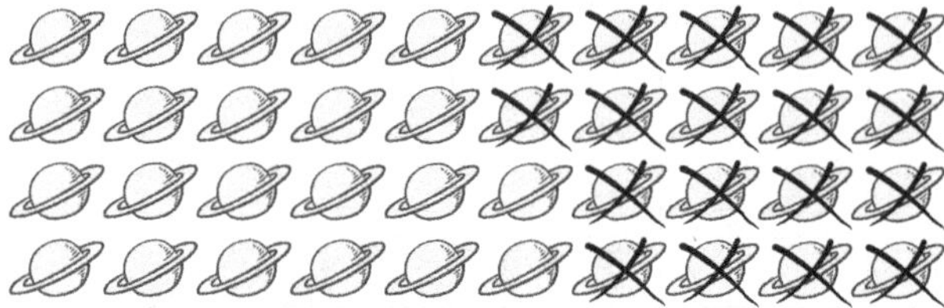

Answer ______________________

6. The Black Mountain is 13,847 feet tall. The Red Mountain is 4,729 feet taller than the Black Mountain. How tall is the Red Mountain?

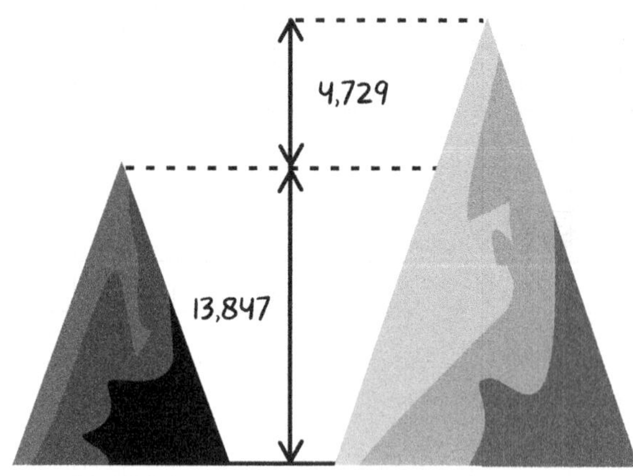

A. 18,576 ft
B. 18,786 ft
C. 18,936 ft
D. 19,116 ft

WEEK 2 DAY 3  MATH

7. There are **266** calories in one **20**-ounce bottle of apple juice. How many calories are there in nine **20**-ounce bottles of apple juice?

A. 1,894 calories
B. 2,164 calories
C. 2,394 calories
D. 2,534 calories

8. Which division problem does the model show?

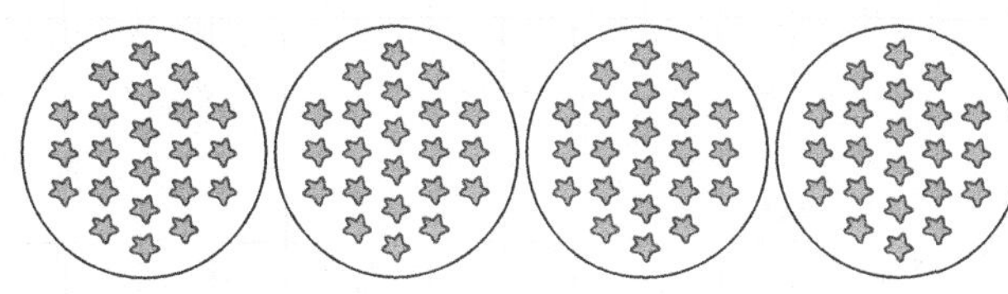

A. 84 ÷ 4
B. 86 ÷ 4
C. 88 ÷ 4
D. 90 ÷ 4

9. What is the difference between 750 and 530? ☆ = 100 and 🪐 = 10.

Answer ______________________

10. What is the sum below times twelve?

× 12

Answer ______________________

FITNESS

☆ Please be aware of your environment and be safe at all times. If you cannot do an exercise, just try your best.

Repeat these exercises **3 ROUNDS**

1 - Bend forward: 10 times.
Note: try to touch your feet. Make sure to keep your back straight and if needed you can bend your knees.

2 - Lunges: 5 times to each leg.
Note: Use your body weight or books as weight to do leg lunges.

3 - Plank: 15 sec.

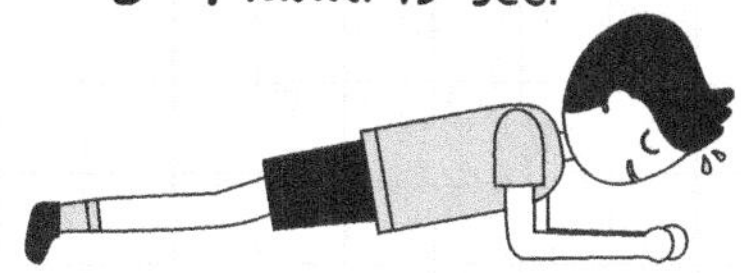

4 - Abs: 10 times

WEEK 2 DAY 4 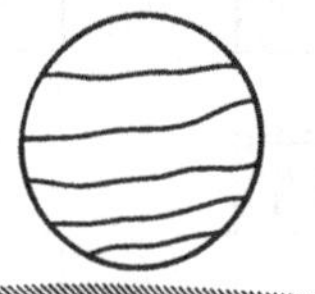 MATH

Place Value

1. In which of the following numbers is the digit 6 in the greatest place value?

   A. 34,679
   B. 26,891
   C. 17,906
   D. 34,765

2. Find and choose a pair of numbers in which the digit 3 differs by a factor of 100.

   A. 34,756 and 23,861
   B. 23,649 and 13,764
   C. 15,239 and 29,763
   D. 37,285 and 86,341

3. James wrote a number on a piece of paper. One of the digits is 9 which is the lowest in value. From the answer choices shown below, which number did James write?

   A. 23,849
   B. 91,756
   C. 17,982
   D. 49,673

4. In what place value is 6 in the number 769,843?

   A. Tens
   B. Hundreds
   C. Thousands
   D. Ten thousands

5. Which digit represents the thousands place in the number 563,947?

   A. 3
   B. 4
   C. 6
   D. 9

6. How many times greater is the number 30,000 than the number 30?

   Answer ____________________

7. The hundreds place value in the number 639,137 is:

   Answer ____________________

8. What is the tens place digit in the number 83,653?

   Answer ____________________

9. Marcus has 7 one hundred dollar bills. How much money does Marcus have?

   Answer ____________________

10. In the number 468,932 the number 4 is in what place value?

    Answer ____________________

Standard form vs expanded form

1. Choose the standard form of the number 6 + 300 + 40,000 + 70 + 8,000

   A. 63,478
   B. 43,876
   C. 48,376
   D. 47,836

WEEK 2 DAY 4  MATH

2. The number 849,362 in expanded form can be written as:

A. 3,000 + 9,000 + 2 + 800,000 + 60 + 40,000
B. 90,000 + 2 + 300 + 40,000 + 800,000 + 60
C. 2 + 9,000 + 800,000 + 60 + 40,000 + 300
D. 600 + 800,000 + 9,000 + 300 + 2 + 40,000

3. Which of the following answer choices represents the number two hundred thousands, six ten thousands, five thousands, four hundreds, three tens, and seven ones in standard form?

A. 264,370
B. 265,473
C. 260,437
D. 265,437

4. What is 600 + 30,000 + 20 + 7,000 + 8 + 900,000 in standard form?

A. 973,628
B. 936,728
C. 937,628
D. 937,682

5. Which combination of numbers is the expanded form of 308,746?

A. 300,000 + 700 +6 + 8,000 + 40
B. 700 + 30,000 + 8,000 + 6 + 40
C. 8,000 + 300,000 + 40 + 7,000 + 6
D. 40 + 700 + 6 + 300,000 + 80,000

6. What is 600 + 40,000 + 3 + 7,000 + 80 + 400,000 in standard form?

Answer ____________________

7. Write the number five ten thousands, four thousands, six hundreds, two tens, and two ones in standard form.

Answer ____________________

8. Rewrite this expanded form from greatest to least: 70 + 50,000 + 300 + 7,000 + 200,000 + 4

Answer ____________________
____

9. Write 700 + 90 + 4,000 + 6 + 60,000 in words.

Answer ____________________
____

FITNESS

Please be aware of your environment and be safe at all times. If you cannot do an exercise, just try your best.

1 - High Plank: 15 sec.

2 - Chair: 20 sec.
Note: sit on an imaginary chair, keep your back straight.

3 - Abs: 10 times

Rounding to the nearest 10, 100 and 1,000

1. Round 679,458 to the nearest thousand.

   A. 679,500
   B. 679,000
   C. 680,000
   D. 680,500

2. Which of the following numbers rounded to the nearest hundred gives you 85,000?

   A. 85,096
   B. 84,972
   C. 84,869
   D. 84,912

3. What is 674,835 rounded to the nearest thousand?

   A. 675,000
   B. 670,000
   C. 680,000
   D. 674,900

4. Choose the number which after rounding to the nearest hundred becomes greater.

   A. 78,349
   B. 86,537
   C. 37,942
   D. 56,471

5. Choose the number which after rounding to the nearest thousand becomes less?

   A. 43,642
   B. 84,471
   C. 35,547
   D. 28,605

6. Round 36,924 to the nearest ten.

   Answer ____________________

7. Which place value do you need to round in the number 56,734 to get 56,700?

   Answer ____________________

8. Round 563,531 to the nearest thousand.

   Answer ____________________

9. Round 67,563 and 67,483 to the nearest ten thousand. Write a number sentence using those two rounded numbers and a comparison symbol.

   Answer ____________________

Problems with fraction comparison

1. Which of the following fractions shown below is 'less' than half?

   A. $\frac{4}{6}$
   B. $\frac{3}{5}$
   C. $\frac{3}{8}$
   D. $\frac{6}{9}$

2. Which number sentence below is true?

   A. $\frac{3}{9} < \frac{4}{6}$
   B. $\frac{5}{8} = \frac{1}{2}$
   C. $\frac{4}{8} > \frac{6}{9}$
   D. $\frac{3}{5} > \frac{4}{6}$

WEEK 2 DAY 5  MATH

3. Which number can be used to make the number sentence true?

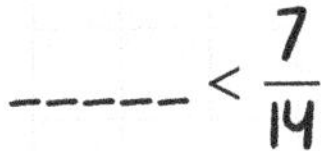

$\_\_\_\_\_ < \frac{7}{14}$

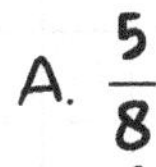

A. $\frac{5}{8}$

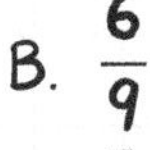

B. $\frac{6}{9}$

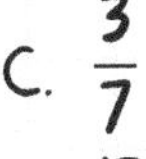

C. $\frac{3}{7}$

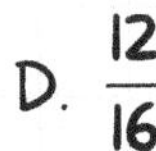

D. $\frac{12}{16}$

4. Which of the following fractions shown below is 'more' than half?

A. $\frac{15}{40}$

B. $\frac{17}{30}$

C. $\frac{23}{49}$

D. $\frac{24}{54}$

5. Randy drank $\frac{3}{5}$ of his milk and Rose drank $\frac{4}{10}$ of her milk. Which statement is true?

A. $\frac{3}{5} < \frac{4}{10}$

B. $\frac{3}{5} = \frac{4}{10}$

C. $\frac{3}{5} > \frac{4}{10}$

D. $\frac{4}{10} > \frac{3}{5}$

6. Use '>' , '<' or '=' for $\frac{5}{12}$ and $\frac{3}{5}$ to create a comparison statement.

Answer ______________________

7. Compare $\frac{6}{12}$ and $\frac{15}{30}$, using '>' , '<' or '='.

Answer ______________________

Please be aware of your environment and be safe at all times. If you cannot do an exercise, just try your best.

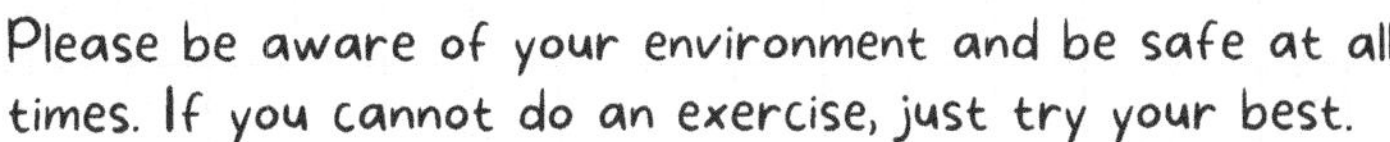

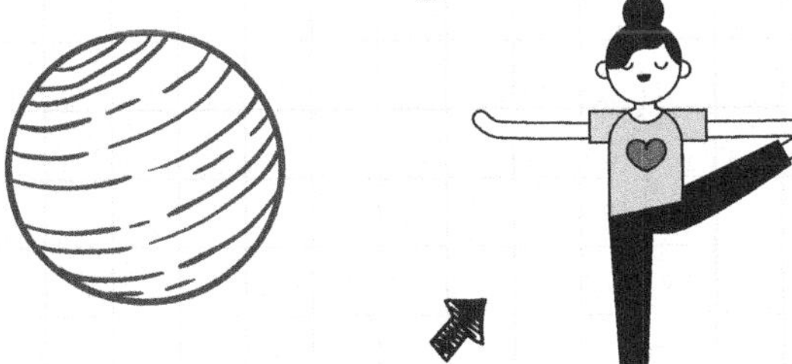

2 - Stretching: Stay as long as possible.
Note: do on one leg then on another.

3 - Lower Plank: 20 sec.
Note: Keep your back straight and body tight.

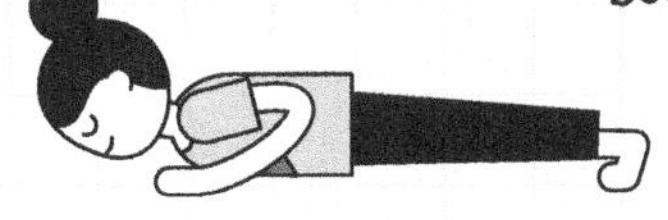

1 - Tree Pose: Stay as long as possible.
Note: do on one leg then on another.

START

5 - Shavasana: 10 min.
Note: this pose is very important and provides you with long term benefits. Try not to skip this. Close your eyes and imagine who you want to be and what your goals are! Always think happy thoughts.

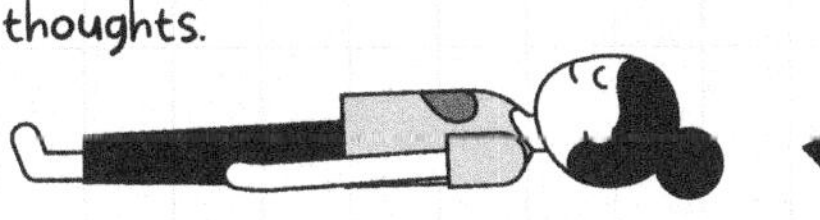

4 - Book Pose: 20 sec.
Note: Keep your core tight. Legs should be across from your eyes.

WEEK 2 DAY 6 EXPERIMENT

Creating Molecules from Elements

Last week, we learned that all matter is made up of **atoms**, which represent the pure building blocks of different **elements**. Atoms of different elements often bond together to form what are known as **compounds**. The most famous and commonplace compound is probably water. There is no such thing as a "water atom" because water is made out of both Hydrogen and Oxygen. Therefore, the most basic unit of a compound is known as a **"molecule"**. Today, we'll take our atom models and build them into some cool molecules.

Materials:

- All 11 atoms created in the "Week 1" activity
- Your notes about the elements from the "Week 1" activity
- 8 wooden skewers or plastic drinking straws
- Scissors
- An encyclopedia or internet access for research

Procedure:

1. Gather the atoms you made last week and separate them out into piles of **Oxygen, Hydrogen, and Carbon** atoms.
2. Take **2 Hydrogen atoms** and **1 Oxygen atom** from the piles, as well as two of your straws or skewers.
3. Take two straws or skewers and insert them into the **Oxygen** atom at the 10 o'clock and 2 o'clock positions on the sphere. You can use your scissors to trim the straws or skewers as needed.
4. Attach a **Hydrogen** atom to the free end of each skewer so you have a three-ball structure that looks a little like a cartoon mouse's head. You've just created a **water molecule**!
5. Using your encyclopedia or internet resources, take 5 minutes to research water and write down **five important facts** on your note sheet, just like you did when you researched the different elements last week.
6. Take **1 Carbon atom** and **2 Oxygen atoms** from the piles, as well as two of your straws or skewers.
7. Take two straws or skewers and insert them into the **Carbon** atom at the 9 o'clock and 3 o'clock positions on the sphere. You can use your scissors to trim the straws or skewers as needed.
8. Attach an **Oxygen** atom to the free end of each skewer so you have a three-ball structure that looks like a stoplight or a caterpillar. You've just created a **Carbon Dioxide molecule**!
9. Using your encyclopedia or internet resources, take 5 minutes to research carbon dioxide and write down **five important facts** on your note sheet, just like you did when you researched the different elements last week.

WEEK 2 DAY 6 EXPERIMENT

10. Take **1 Carbon atom** and **4 Hydrogen atoms** from the piles, as well as four of your straws or skewers.
11. Take four straws or skewers and insert them into the **Carbon** atom at the 12 o'clock, 3 o'clock, 6 o'clock, and 9 o'clock positions on the sphere. You can use your scissors to trim the straws or skewers as needed.
12. Attach a **Hydrogen** atom to the free end of each skewer so you have a five-ball structure. You've just created a **Methane molecule**!
13. Using your encyclopedia or internet resources, take 5 minutes to research Methane and write down **five important facts** on your note sheet, just like you did when you researched the different elements last week.
14. After you've created and researched your molecules, be sure to hang onto your notes and your models, since we'll be using them next week as well.

Follow-Up Questions:

1. Carbon dioxide and water are pretty well-known, but Methane is a little more complex. What was the most interesting thing you learned about Methane?

____

____

____

2. What do you think the straws or skewers in the models represent?

____

____

____

YOGA

Please be aware of your environment and be safe at all times. If you cannot do an exercise, just try your best.

1 - Bend Down: 20 sec.

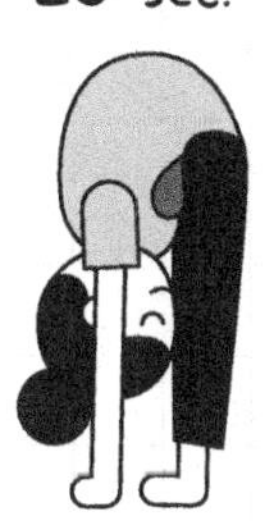

2 - Chair: 20 sec.

3 - Child Pose: 20 sec.

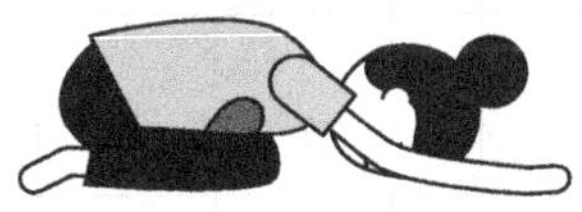

4 - Shavasana: as long as you can. Note: think of happy moments and relax your mind.

WEEK 2 DAY 7  MAZE

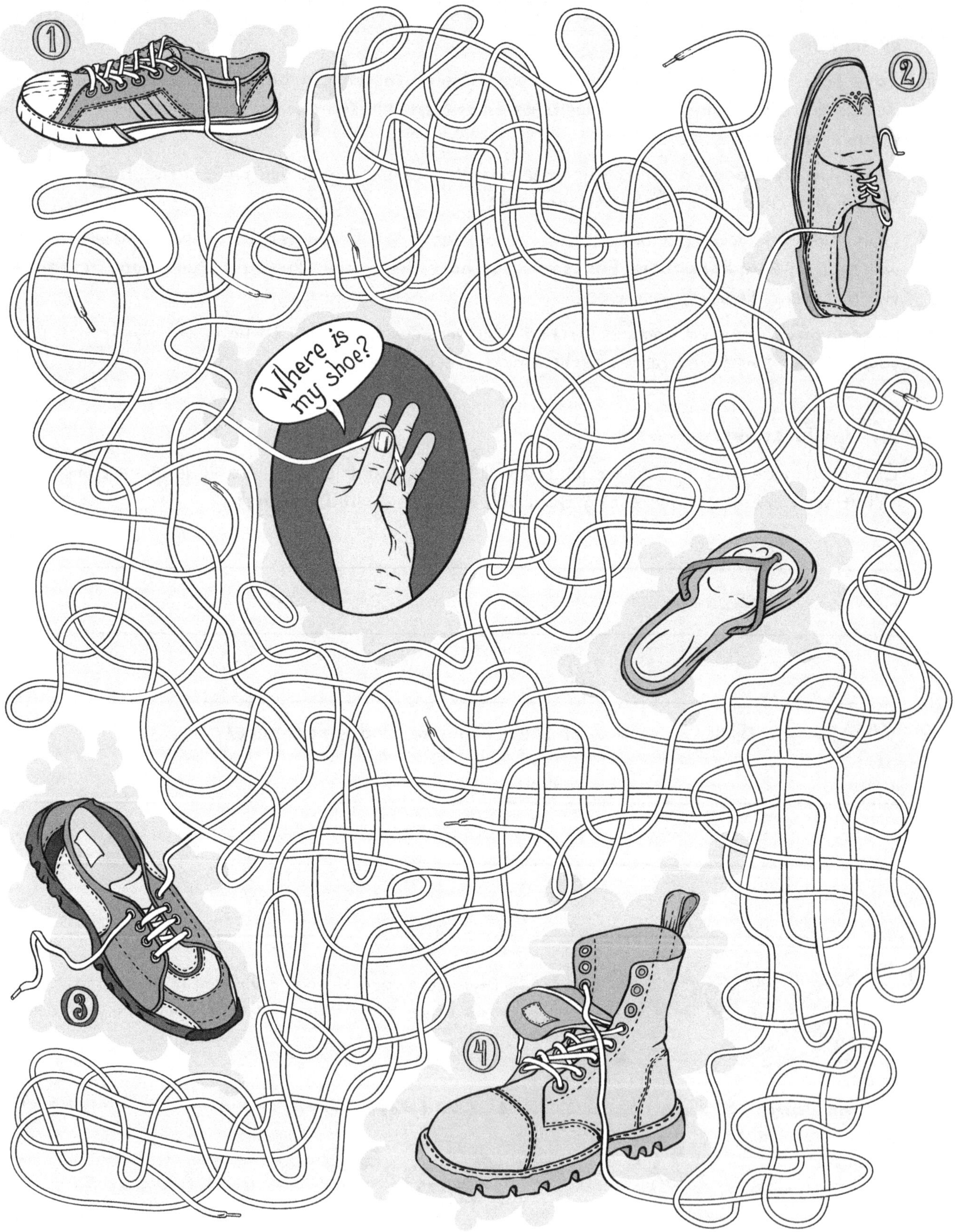

1

2

Where is my shoe?

3

4

Answer: ______________________

That's what I'm talking about!

You did a great job.
Now we can stop at planet Earth
and learn some fun facts.

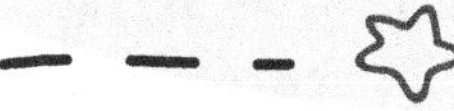

70% of the Earth's surface is covered in water

When astronauts first went into space and saw Earth from up above for the first time, they called our home the Blue Planet.

WEEK 3 DAY 1  OVERVIEW OF ENGLISH CONCEPTS TRANSITION WORDS

Part of being a good writer is providing your readers with a **smooth, easy reading experience** that makes it really simple for them to understand what you're talking about and how your thoughts and writing are organized. One of the most effective ways to provide clarity for your reader is by incorporating **transition words** into your writing.

Transitions help your reader recognize when you're making a new or different point and also communicate **the relationships between ideas**. It's important to choose the right transition word to communicate the relationship between the sentence or paragraph you just finished and the one you're about to start.

For Example...

Transition	Relationship it Communicates	Example
For example	The next sentence or phrase is an **example** that illustrates what came before it.	Our shirts are available in a variety of colors and styles. **For example**, we have long and short-sleeved t-shirts in red, blue, green, and purple.
Furthermore	The next sentence or phrase will **reinforce** or **back up** the one that came before it.	The plan to close the library will hurt our community because many people use that space to read and study. **Furthermore**, the library provides great after-school programs to children in our town.
However	The next sentence or phrase will **contradict** or **disagree** with the ideas that came before it.	Darcy thought Jack was hiding in the tree. When she climbed to the top, **however**, she realized he wasn't there.
Subsequently	The next sentence or idea happened **after** the event in the previous sentence.	We went to the grocery store and bought ten pounds of beans. **Subsequently**, we made a big batch of chili.
Consequently	The next sentence or idea happened **as a direct consequence** of the events in the previous sentence.	I rode my bike through the red light. **Consequently**, an officer pulled me over and wrote me a ticket.

From "Welsh Fairy Tales"

By William Elliot Griffis

After the Cymric folk, that is, the people we call Welsh, had come up from Cornwall into their new land, they began to cut down the trees, to build towns, and to have fields and gardens. Soon they made the landscape smile with pleasant homes, rich farms and playing children.

They trained vines and made flowers grow. The young folks made pets of the wild animals' cubs, which their fathers and big brothers brought home from hunting. Old men took rushes and reeds and wove them into cages for song birds to live in.

While they were draining the swamps and bogs, they drove out the monsters that had made their lair in these wet places. These terrible creatures liked to poison people with their bad breath, and even ate up very little boys and girls, when they strayed away from home.

So all the face of the open country between the forests became very pretty to look at. The whole of Cymric land, which then extended from the northern Grampian Hills to Cornwall, and from the Irish Sea, past their big fort, afterward called London, even to the edge of the German Ocean, became a delightful place to live in.

The lowlands and the rivers, in which the tide rose and fell daily, were especially attractive. This was chiefly because of the many bright flowers growing there; while the yellow gorse and the pink heather made the hills look as lovely as a young girl's face. Besides this, the Cymric maidens were the prettiest ever, and the lads were all brave and healthy; while both of these knew how to sing often and well.

1. Based on the passage, how would you describe Cymric life and culture?

___

___

2. Which aspects of this story seem like they are definitely **embellished** or **stretching the truth**?

___

___

___

___

3. Which of these words or phrases would provide the **strongest transition** into Paragraph 5?

   A. Unfortunately
   B. Luckily
   C. Consequently
   D. For example

4. The author uses the **transition** "Besides this" in Paragraph 5 to mean the same thing as which of these words?

   A. However
   B. Subsequently
   C. Additionally
   D. First

5. Based on how incredibly beautiful and perfect this place is described as being, what do you predict will happen next in the story?

____

____

____

____

____

____

Identifying and Explaining Transitions

Directions:

Circle the transition word in each group of sentences below. Then, on the lines below the sentence, explain what that transition word tells you about the relationship between the two sentences.

1. Marco and Irene are both great spellers. Regrettably, only one of them can win the school spelling bee.

2. Our bus got held up at the tracks while a long freight train passed. Consequently, we were all late for school.

3. There are several good reasons why students at the high school should be able to leave campus to get lunch. First of all, there are many great and affordable restaurants nearby.

4. Petra and Molly got caught talking during an important test. Of course, Mr. Harrison gave them detention.

5. Rudy loves to pull pranks on people. For the most part, it's all harmless fun.

FITNESS

☆ Please be aware of your environment and be safe at all times. If you cannot do an exercise, just try your best.

1 - Bend forward: 10 times.
Note: try to touch your feet. Make sure to keep your back straight and if needed you can bend your knees.

2 - Abs: 10 times

3 - Plank: 15 sec.

4 - Run: 50 m
Note: Run 25 meters to one side and 25 meters back to the starting position.

From "Welsh Fairy Tales"

By William Elliot Griffis

(Continued from Day 1's Passage)

Now there was a great monster named the Afang, that lived in a big bog, hidden among the high hills and inside of a dark, rough forest.

This ugly creature had an iron-clad back and a long tail that could wrap itself around a mountain. It had four front legs, with big knees that were bent up like a grasshopper's, but were covered with scales like armor. These were as hard as steel, and bulged out at the thighs. Along its back, was a ridge of horns, like spines, and higher than an alligator's. Against such a tough hide, when the hunters shot their darts and hurled their javelins, these weapons fell down to the ground, like harmless pins.

On this monster's head, were big ears, half way between those of a donkey and an elephant. Its eyes were as green as leeks, and were round, but scalloped on the edges, like squashes, while they were as big as pumpkins.

The Afang's face was much like a monkey's, or a gorilla's, with long straggling gray hairs around its cheeks like those of a walrus. It always looked as if a napkin, as big as a bath towel, would be necessary to keep its mouth clean. Yet even then, it slobbered a good deal, so that no nice fairy liked to be near the monster.

When the Afang growled, the bushes shook and the oak leaves trembled on the branches, as if a strong wind was blowing.

But after its dinner, when it had swallowed down a man, or two calves, or four sheep, or a fat heifer, or three goats, its body swelled up like a balloon. Then it usually rolled over, lay along the ground, or in the soft mud, and felt very stupid and sleepy, for a long while.

All around its lair, lay wagon loads of bones of the creatures, girls, women, men, boys, cows, and occasionally a donkey, which it had devoured.

But when the Afang was ravenously hungry and could not get these animals and when fat girls and careless boys were scarce, it would live on birds, beasts and fishes. Although it was very fond of cows and sheep, yet the wool and hair of these animals stuck in its big teeth, it often felt very miserable and its usually bad temper grew worse.

WEEK 3 DAY 2 READING PASSAGE TRANSITION WORDS

1. How is the content of this passage significantly different from the content of the Day 1 passage (which comes right before it)?

____

____

2. Which details from the description of the Afang help establish that the monster is terrifying?

____

____

____

____

3. Which **transition** word could the author use instead of "but" at the beginning of Paragraph 6?

   A. For example
   B. Moreover
   C. However
   D. Subsequently

4. Which **transition** word could the author use instead of "Yet even then" at the end of Paragraph 4?

   A. In spite of this
   B. Consequently
   C. However
   D. Finally

5. Based on what you read on Day 1 and what you read today, what do you predict is going to happen next in this story? What makes you say that?

____

____

____

____

WEEK 3 DAY 2 ACTIVITIES TRANSITION WORDS

Choosing the Best Transition for a Situation

Directions:

Read the pair of sentences and circle the transition in parentheses that would best go in the blank to show the relationships between ideas.

1. I expected our trip to the museum to be boring. __________________, it turned out to be the most fun I've had in a long time. (MOREOVER / HOWEVER / ADDITIONALLY)

2. My brother and I have a great relationship, and I love him very much. __________________, I think he is behaving like a total moron right now. (WITH THAT BEING SAID / FOR EXAMPLE / IN CONCLUSION)

3. The study of history is important because it helps you understand how people from the past approached similar social situations to what we are experiencing today. __________________, if we study history closely, we can try to avoid making the same mistakes as our ancestors. (SIMILARLY / UNFORTUNATELY / ADDITIONALLY)

4. There are many reasons our town needs to raise taxes. __________________, the main roads are all filled with potholes. (TO BE HONEST / CONSEQUENTLY / FOR EXAMPLE)

5. Make sure to lock the back door before you go to bed. __________________, someone might be able to get into the house. (OTHERWISE / THEREFORE / HOWEVER)

FITNESS

Please be aware of your environment and be safe at all times. If you cannot do an exercise, just try your best.

Repeat these exercises **3 ROUNDS**

1 - Squats: 15 times. Note: imagine you are trying to sit on a chair.

2 - Side Bending: 10 times to each side. Note: try to touch your feet.

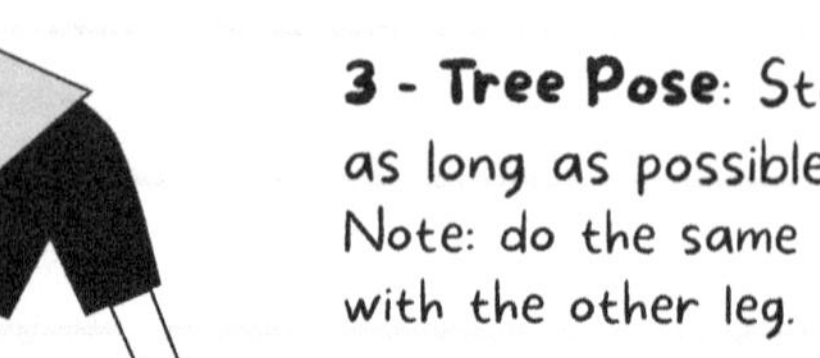

3 - Tree Pose: Stay as long as possible. Note: do the same with the other leg.

Problems with fractions and diagrams

1. Which statement is represented by the model below.

A. $\frac{7}{12} = \frac{4}{6}$

B. $\frac{7}{12} > \frac{4}{6}$

C. $\frac{7}{12} < \frac{4}{6}$

D. $\frac{4}{6} < \frac{7}{12}$

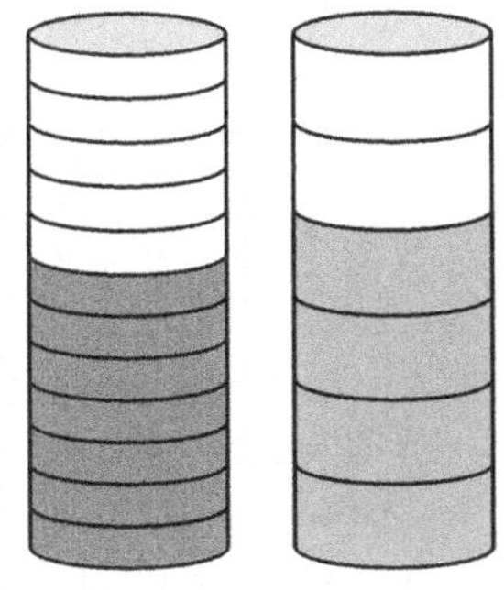

2. What fraction represents the shaded circles in the model?

A. $\frac{6}{18}$

B. $\frac{6}{24}$

C. $\frac{18}{24}$

D. $\frac{6}{20}$

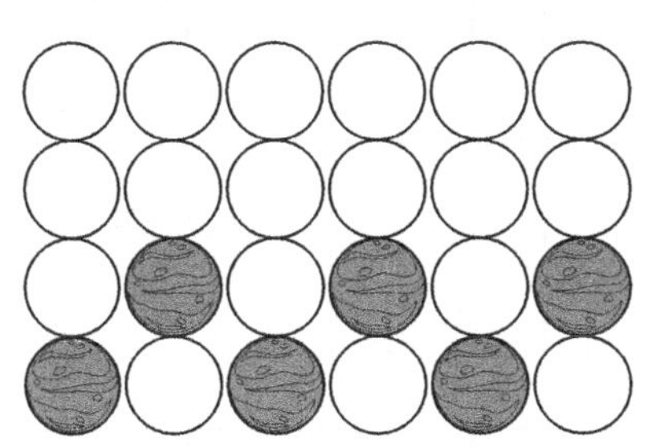

3. Which fraction is equal to the shaded part in the model below?

A. $\frac{2}{3}$

B. $\frac{9}{15}$

C. $\frac{5}{8}$

D. $\frac{6}{8}$

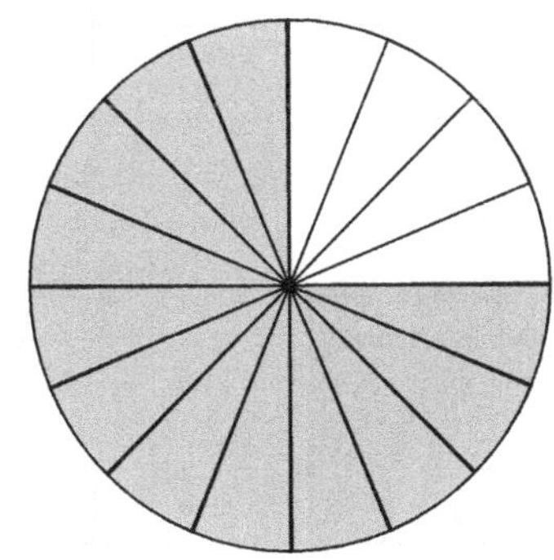

4. Determine if the shaded amount is "less", "more" or "equal to" half.

Answer ______________________

5. What fraction represents the shaded portion of the model shown below?

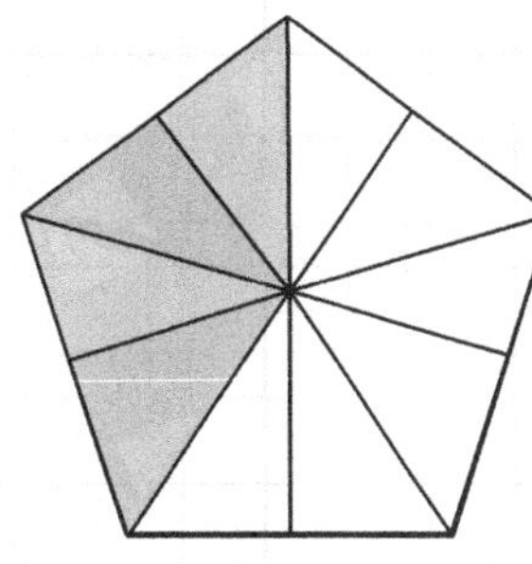

A. $\frac{4}{10}$ or one fourth

B. $\frac{4}{10}$ or four tenths

C. $\frac{2}{5}$ or one fifth

D. $\frac{4}{5}$ or four fifths

6. Fill in the empty boxes with fractions that are represented on the number line.

Answer ______________________

7. Write a fraction that represents the shaded portion of the model below.

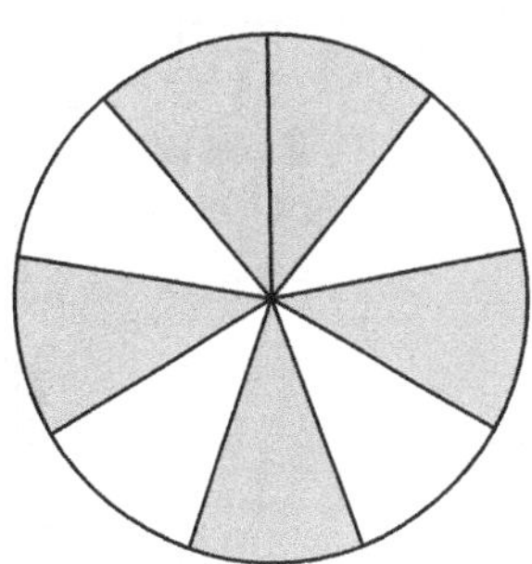

Answer ______________________

8. Which model is equal to the fraction $\frac{6}{16}$?

A.

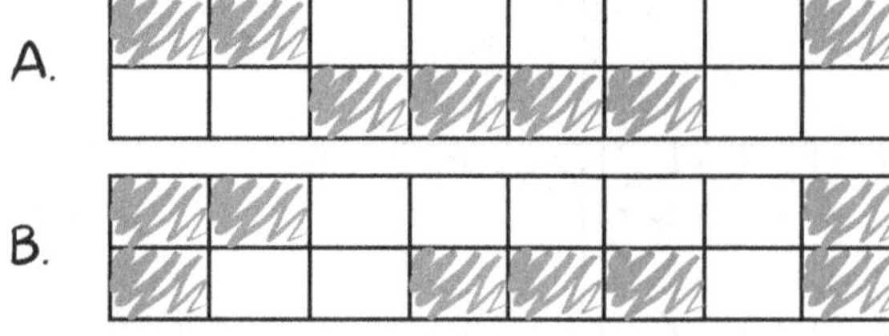

B.

C.

D.

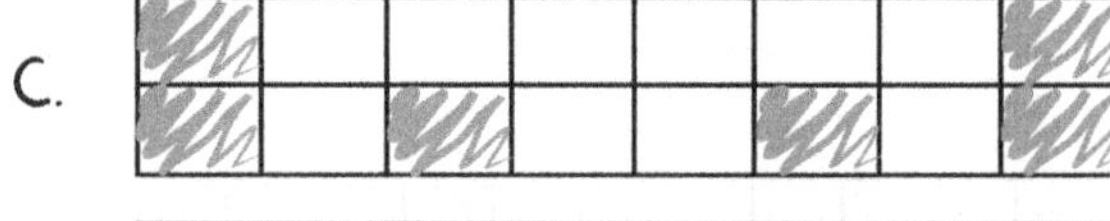

Answer ____________________

9. Determine which shaded amount is 'less' than half.

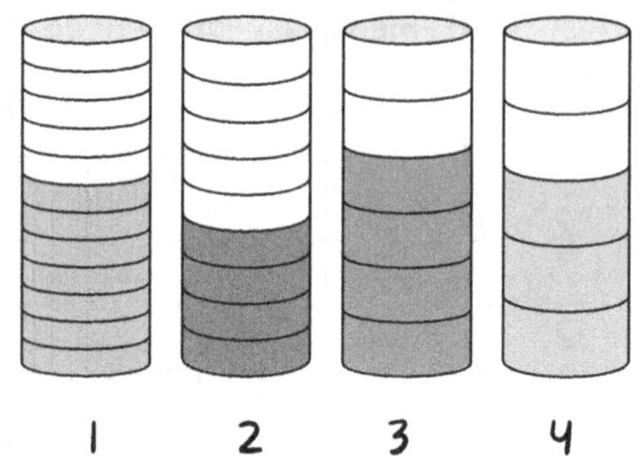

Answer ____________________

10. Complete the statement represented by the model below.

$\frac{?}{16} = \frac{5}{?}$

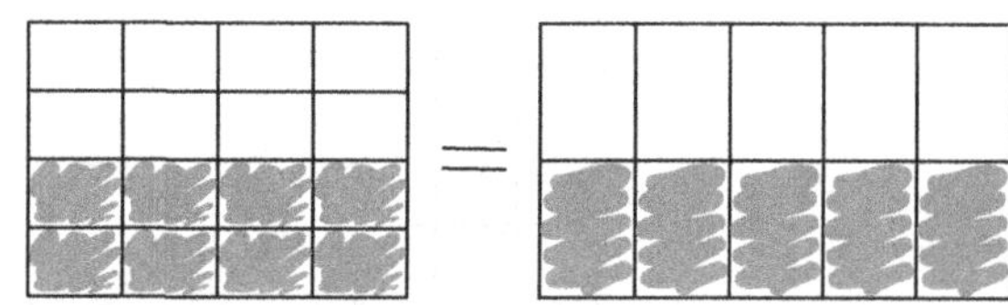

Answer ____________________

FITNESS

Please be aware of your environment and be safe at all times. If you cannot do an exercise, just try your best.

Repeat these exercises **3 ROUNDS**

1 - Bend forward: 10 times.
Note: try to touch your feet. Make sure to keep your back straight and if needed you can bend your knees.

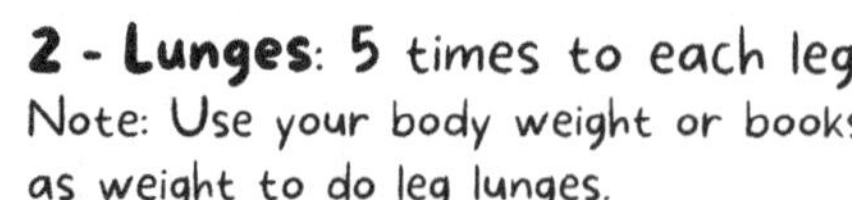

2 - Lunges: 5 times to each leg.
Note: Use your body weight or books as weight to do leg lunges.

3 - Plank: 15 sec.

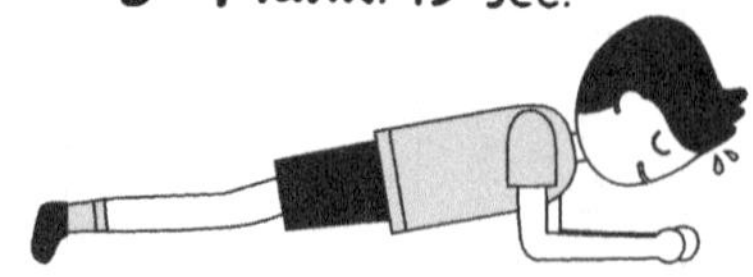

4 - Abs: 10 times

Shading in fraction models

1. How can we calculate the shaded area?

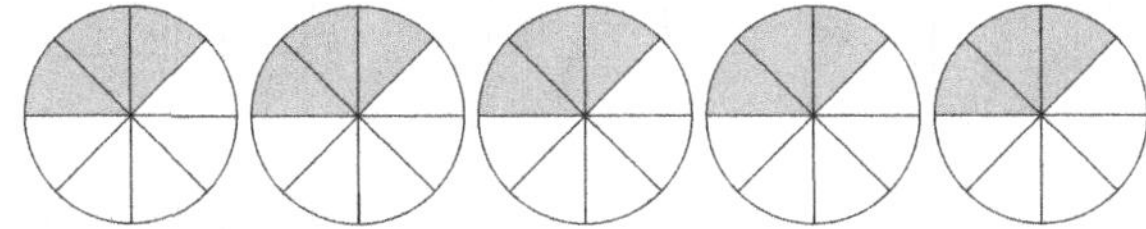

Answer ______________________

2. Which number sentence represents the amount of the fraction model that is shaded?

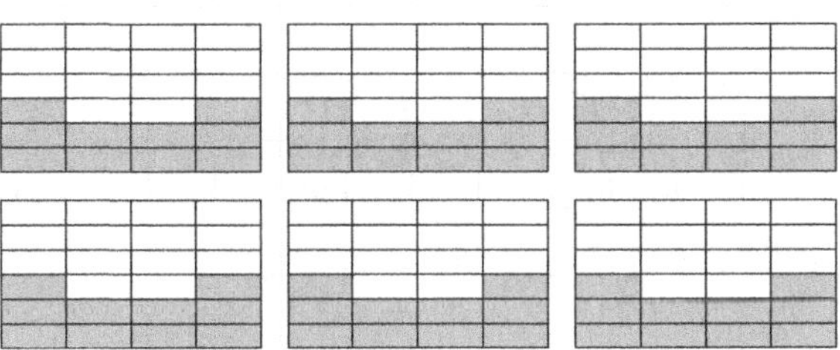

A. $6 + \frac{10}{24} = \frac{60}{24}$

B. $6 \times \frac{10}{14} = \frac{60}{14}$

C. $6 \times \frac{10}{24} = \frac{60}{24}$

D. $6 \times \frac{14}{10} = \frac{84}{10}$

3. What fraction represents the shaded portion for the model shown below?

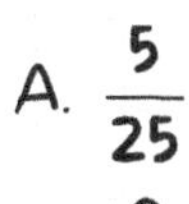
A. $\frac{5}{25}$

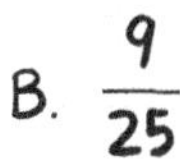
B. $\frac{9}{25}$

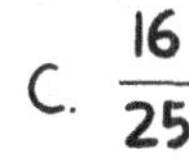
C. $\frac{16}{25}$

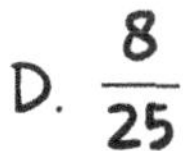
D. $\frac{8}{25}$

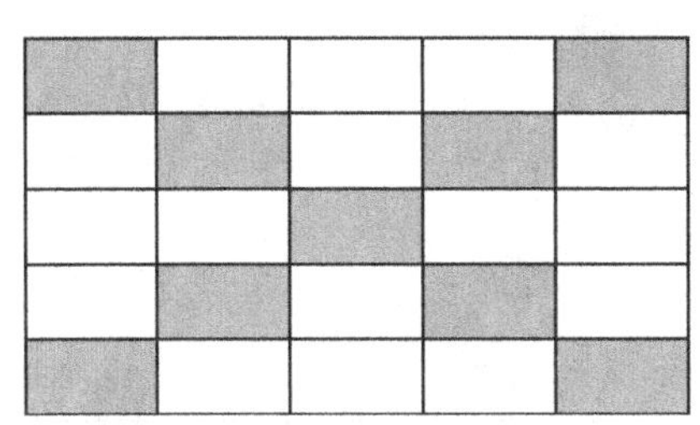

4. Which model represents the fraction $\frac{6}{11}$?

A.
B.
C.
D.

5. How can we calculate the shaded area using a series of fractions?

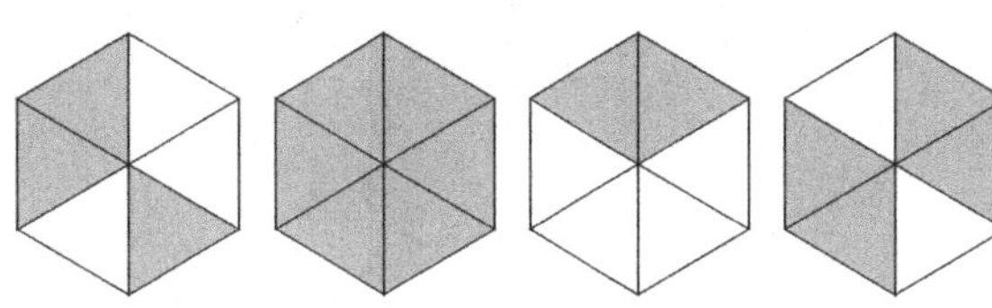

Answer ______________________

6. Which number sentence represents the amount of the fraction model that is shaded?

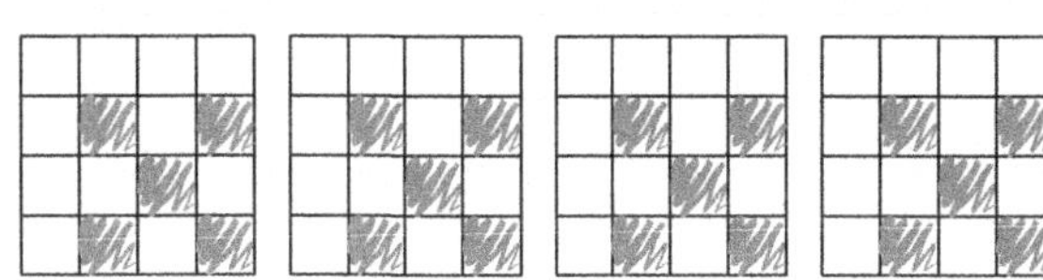

A. $\frac{5}{16} + 4 = 4\frac{5}{16}$

B. $\frac{11}{16} \times 4 = \frac{44}{16}$

C. $\frac{5}{11} \times 4 = \frac{20}{11}$

D. $\frac{5}{16} \times 4 = 1\frac{4}{16}$

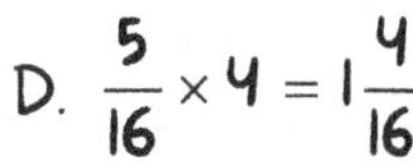

7. Which fraction $\frac{3}{8}$ or $\frac{8}{16}$ is greater? Show your answer, using an inequality symbol.

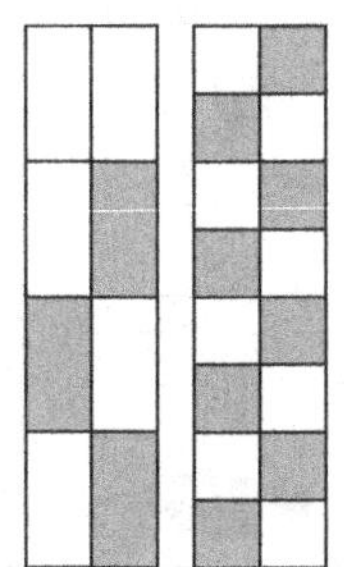

Answer ___________

8. Find the equation modeled below.

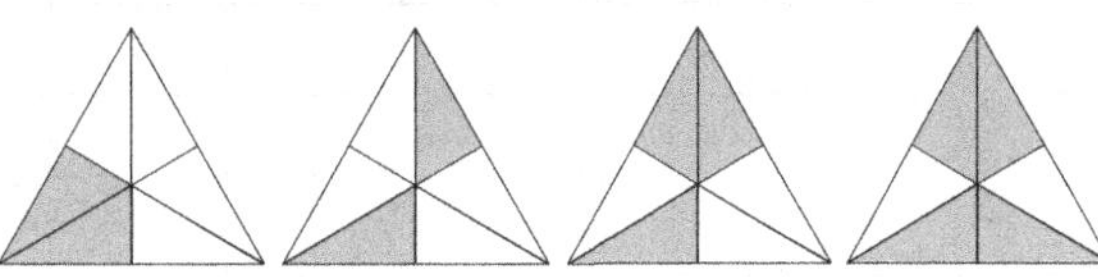

A. $\frac{2}{6} \times 4 = 1\frac{2}{6}$

B. $\frac{2}{6} + \frac{2}{6} + \frac{4}{6} + \frac{4}{6} = \frac{12}{6}$

C. $\frac{2}{6} + \frac{2}{6} + \frac{3}{6} + \frac{4}{6} = 1\frac{5}{6}$

D. $\frac{2}{6} + 2 + \frac{3}{6} + \frac{4}{6} = 3\frac{3}{6}$

9. Using the shaded area in the model below, find $1\frac{14}{20} - \frac{19}{20}$.

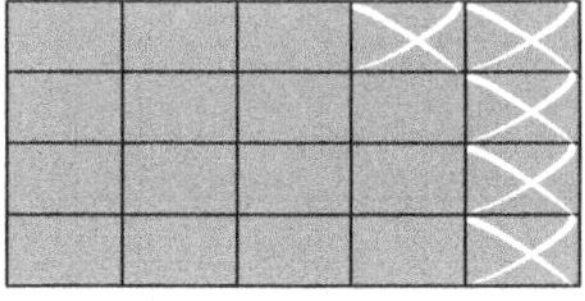 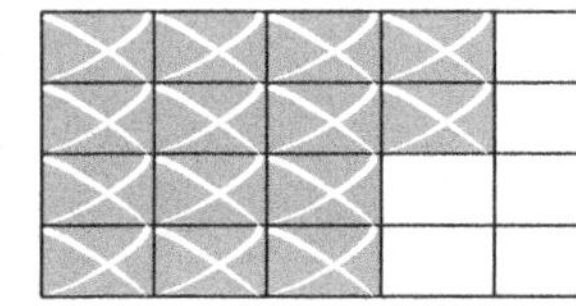

Answer ____________________

10. Write a fraction that represents the shaded portion on the model shown below.

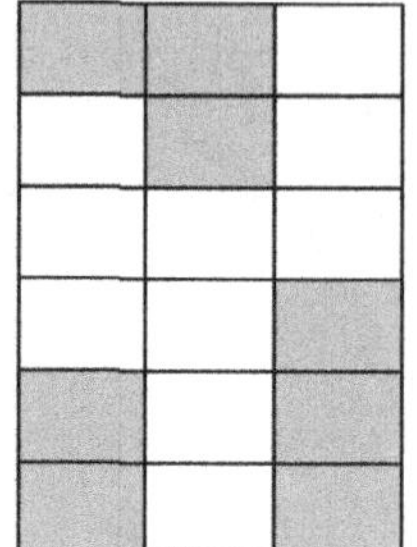

Answer __________

Comparing numbers using comparison symbols (<, >, =)

1. Which expression is true?

A. 245,867 > 245,871
B. 23,954 < 23,934
C. 675,123 > 674,567
D. 82,732 < 82,639

2. Which number can be used to make the number sentence true?

_____ < 24,786

A. 24,805
B. 24,779
C. 24,936
D. 24,789

FITNESS

Please be aware of your environment and be safe at all times. If you cannot do an exercise, just try your best.

Repeat these exercises **3 ROUNDS**

1 - High Plank: 15 sec.

2 - Chair: 20 sec.
Note: sit on an imaginary chair, keep your back straight.

3 - Abs: 10 times

4 - Side Bending: 10 times to each side.
Note: try to touch your feet.

Comparing numbers using comparison symbols (<, >, =)

1. Which symbol would make this inequality true?

   659,123 ____ 658,989

   A. >
   B. <
   C. =
   D. +

2. Compare the numbers 47,932 and 47,899, using a comparison symbol.

   Answer ______________________

3. Write a true number sentence using a comparison symbol and the numbers 68,534 and 68,542.

   Answer ______________________

4. Make a true number sentence using a comparison symbol and the numbers 246,537 and 245,589.

   Answer ______________________

5. Compare the sums of 34,276 + 45,268 and 53,185 + 26,359.

   Answer ______________________

6. Round 8,761 and 8,834 to the nearest hundred. Write a true number statement using the rounded numbers and a comparison symbol.

   Answer ______________________

7. Compare the differences of 34,296 - 25,168 and 76,352 - 65,325.

   Answer ______________________

8. Compare $\frac{7}{9}$ and $\frac{10}{18}$, using '>', '<' or '='.

   Answer ______________________

Area and perimeter

1. What is the area of the rectangle?

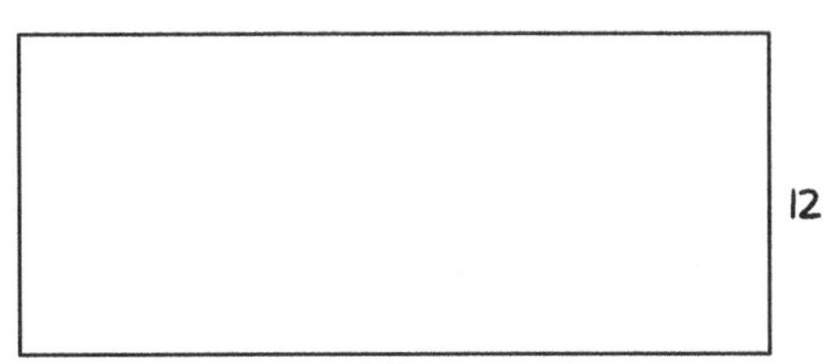

28 in

   A. 336 sq in
   B. 338 sq in
   C. 342 sq in
   D. 348 sq in

2. Find the perimeter of the rhombus.

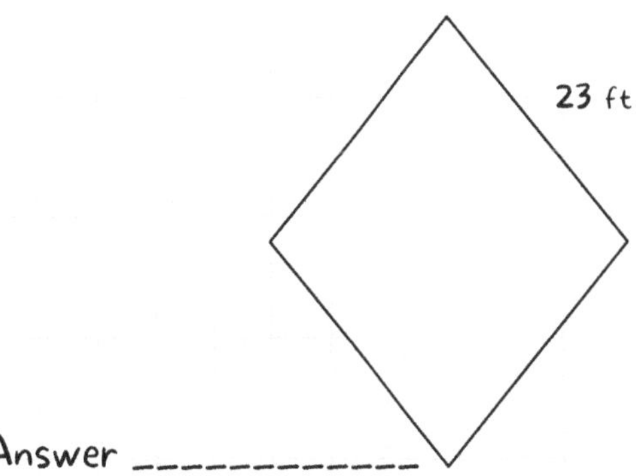

   Answer ____________

3. The perimeter of a rectangle is 60 cm. The length is 4 times as long as its width. Find the width of the rectangle.

   A. 4 cm
   B. 5 cm
   C. 6 cm
   D. 8 cm

WEEK 3 DAY 5  MATH

4. The perimeter of a rectangle is 346 inches. The length is 98 inches. What is the area of the rectangle?

   A. 6,805 sq in
   B. 7,350 sq in
   C. 8,358 sq in
   D. 8,136 sq in

5. The perimeter of a square is 128 centimeters. What is the area of the square?

   A. 954 sq cm
   B. 1,164 sq cm
   C. 834 sq cm
   D. 1,024 sq cm

6. Find the area and the perimeter of the shape below.

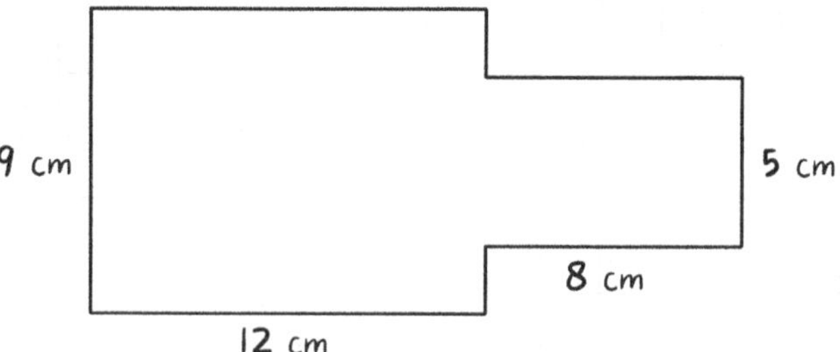

Answer ____________________

7. The perimeter of a square is 144 feet. How long is each side?

Answer ____________________

8. The area of the rectangle is 72 square meters. The length is 12 meters. What is the width of a rectangle?

Answer ____________________

9. A rectangle is 32 inches wide. The length is 3 times as long as its width. Find the perimeter of this rectangle.

Answer ____________________

10. Find the area and the perimeter of the shape below.

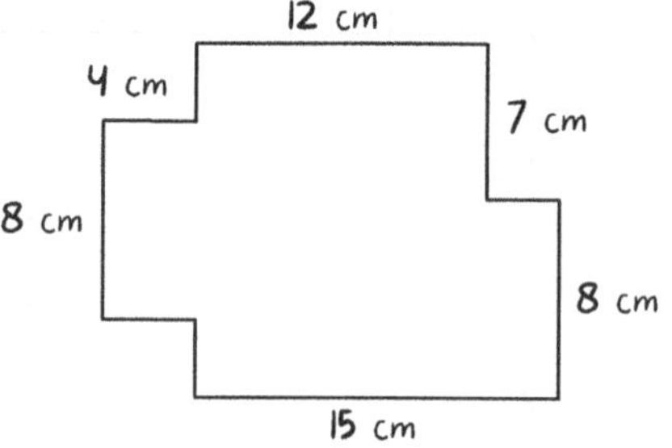

Answer ____________________

YOGA

Please be aware of your environment and be safe at all times. If you cannot do an exercise, just try your best.

1 - Bend Down: 20 sec.

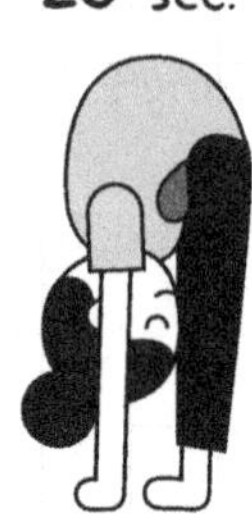

2 - Chair: 20 sec.

3 - Child Pose: 20 sec.

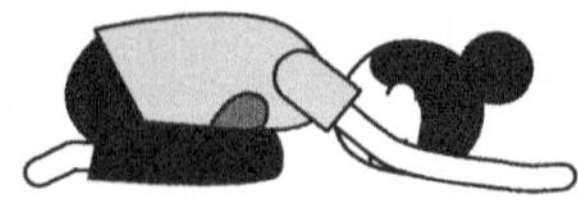

4 - Shavasana: as long as you can. Note: think of happy moments and relax your mind.

WEEK 3 DAY 6 EXPERIMENT

Observing the Conservation of Matter

Over the last few weeks, we've explored how everything is made up of **matter**. The smallest units of matter are known as **atoms**, which represent certain elements. Where atoms of different elements combine to form something new, it is known as a **compound**. The smallest units of a compound are known as **molecules**.

Atoms and molecules can interact, join up, and combine to form new and different **compounds**, but it's important to know that **atoms are never created or destroyed**, they simply bond together in different ways. This principle is known as the **conservation of matter**. Today, we'll see the **conservation of matter** in action by rearranging our molecules.

Materials:

- The **Water, Carbon Dioxide, and Methane molecules** you created last week
- Your notepaper with research from the last two weeks
- An encyclopedia or internet access for research
- 8 wooden skewers or plastic drinking straws

Procedure:

1. Begin by carefully taking apart the molecules you've created. Remove the skewers or straws and set them aside in a pile and sort the different atoms into piles as well.
2. Take the two **Carbon** atoms (one from the **Carbon Dioxide** molecule and one from the **Methane** molecule) and, using a skewer or straw, attach them side-by-side.
3. Next, take your six **Hydrogen** atoms and organize them into two piles of three.
4. Take three **Hydrogen** atoms and, using skewers or straws, attach them to the **Carbon** atom on the left at the 11 o'clock, 9 o'clock, and 7 o'clock positions on the sphere.
5. Take the three remaining **Hydrogen** atoms and, using skewers or straws, attach them to the **Carbon** atom on the right at the 1 o'clock, 3 o'clock, and 5 o'clock positions. You've just created an **Ethane molecule**, which should have 2 Carbon atoms and 6 Hydrogen atoms!
6. Using your encyclopedia or internet resources, take 5 minutes to research Ethane and write down **five important facts** on your note sheet, just like you did when you researched the different elements last week.
7. Take a look at the pile of Styrofoam balls you didn't use. You should have 3 **Oxygen atoms**. These atoms represent the **conservation of matter** because, even though we took atoms from water, Carbon Dioxide, and Methane to make our Ethane gas, there is still remaining oxygen that we didn't use. Since matter is never truly created or destroyed, those atoms would join with others to form new compounds.

WEEK 3 DAY 6 EXPERIMENT

Follow-Up Questions:

1. How did reorganizing your **molecules** illustrate the **conservation of matter**?

2. What's one example of a situation you can think of in which matter **appears** to be getting destroyed (even though it **isn't**)?

YOGA

Please be aware of your environment and be safe at all times. If you cannot do an exercise, just try your best.

2 - Down Dog: 20 sec.

3 - Stretching: Stay as long as possible. Note: do on one leg then on another.

4 - Lower Plank: 20 sec. Note: Keep your back straight and body tight.

1 - Tree Pose: Stay as long as possible. Note: do on one leg then on another.

START

6 - Shavasana: 10 min. Note: this pose is very important and provides you with long term benefits. Try not to skip this. Close your eyes and imagine who you want to be and what your goals are! Always think happy thoughts.

5 - Book Pose: 20 sec. Note: Keep your core tight. Legs should be across from your eyes.

WEEK 3 DAY 7 MAZE

Task: For a clean, healthy mouth, taking two minutes twice a day to brush your teeth isn't a bad trade-off. Find and connect the right tube to the toothbrush.

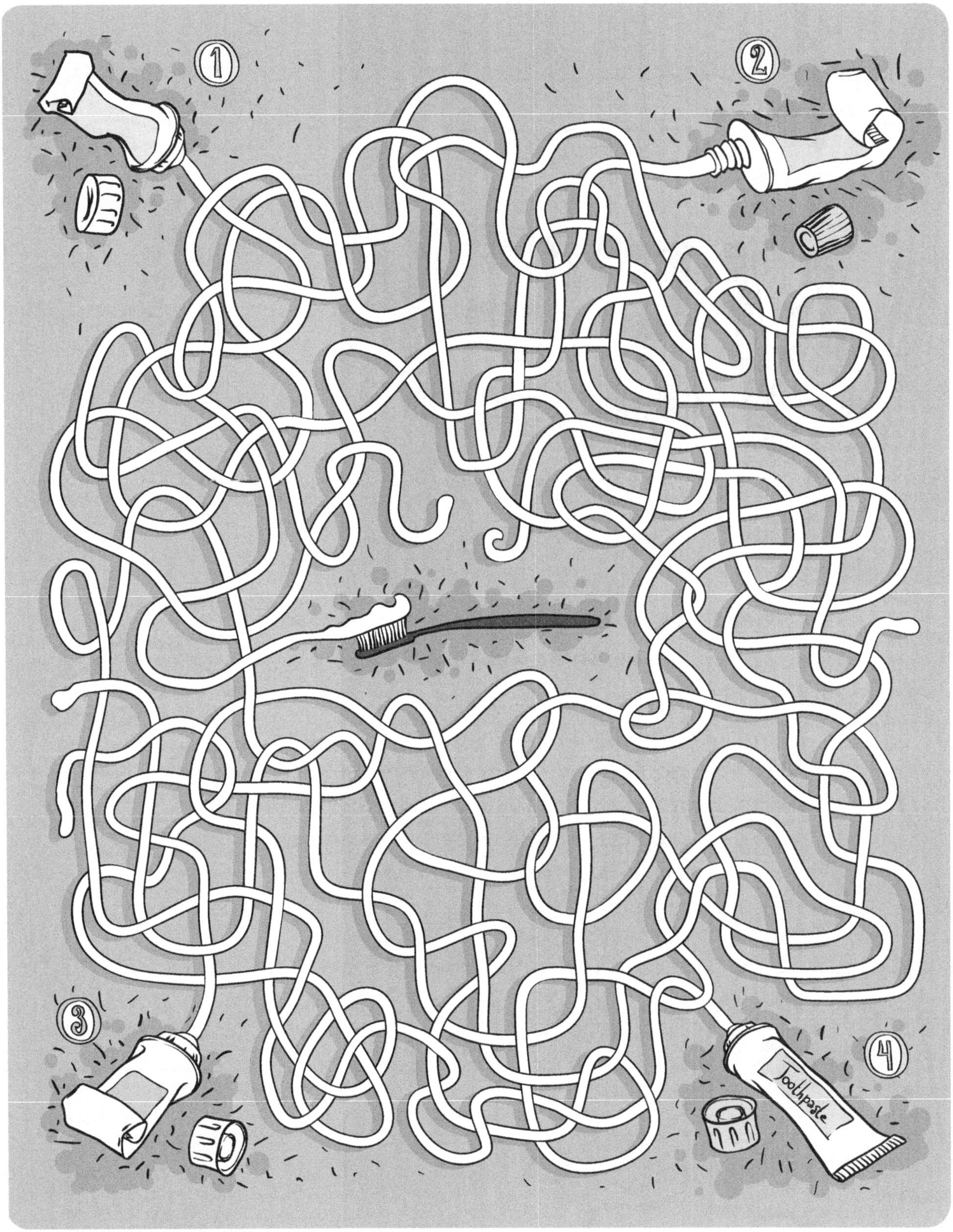

1 2 3 4

Toothpaste

Answer: _______________________

Rock on!
So you're ready to learn
about planet Mars?
WEEK 4
Mars has the largest dust storms in
the solar system.
The harsh dust storms on Mars can last
for months and even cover the entire planet.
Why is it so extreme? Mars has an elliptical
shape for its path around the sun. Compared
to other planets, this elongated path causes
extreme dust storms on Mars.

WEEK 4 DAY 1

OVERVIEW OF ENGLISH CONCEPTS
CLEAR, ORGANIZED PARAGRAPH STRUCTURE

Now that you're capable of writing more advanced sentences that communicate ideas effectively and precisely, it's time to talk about putting sentences together in a **paragraph**. In order to give your reader a straightforward, easy-to-follow reading experience, you must provide them with **structure and organization**.

When you write a paragraph, that paragraph should be **focused on one major topic or idea.** That topic should be communicated to the reader clearly in the **first** sentence of the paragraph. We call that first sentence a **topic sentence**. The sentences in the middle of the paragraph should contain **details, examples, evidence, and explanations** of what you're talking about. We call that part of the paragraph the **body**. The body is where you make most of your actual points. Finally, you should wrap up your paragraphs by **summarizing** your main idea for the reader or **reminding them** what the whole point of the paragraph was. We call that a **conclusion sentence**.

As you read, it's important to begin thinking about what each sentence's role is in its paragraph, as well as what each paragraph's role is in the overall essay or story. When you start to understand the jobs that sentences and paragraphs are performing, you're growing as both a reader and a writer.

Key Terms

Topic Sentence: The first sentence in a paragraph that tells the reader the topic.

Conclusion Sentence: The last sentence in a paragraph that summarizes or wraps up the paragraph for the reader.

Body: The sentences and ideas that come between the topic sentence and the conclusion. The place where you present your ideas, examples, and supporting points.

For Example...

Mr. Stevens is a really great social studies teacher. Kids love his class because he always makes learning fun by using humor and interesting visual aids. His students also appreciate that Mr. Stevens never gives more than fifteen minutes of homework because he wants kids to have time to relax away from school, as long as they try their hardest during class. When it's time for tests and quizzes, he also lets kids retake anything lower than a B to boost their final grade and show they truly understand the material. For all those reasons, Mr. Stevens is the most popular teacher in school.

WEEK 4 DAY 1  OVERVIEW OF ENGLISH CONCEPTS

CLEAR, ORGANIZED PARAGRAPH STRUCTURE

Topic Sentence: Mr. Stevens is a really great social studies teacher

- Tells the reader the paragraph is about **Mr. Stevens** and the idea that he's a **great teacher.**

Body Sentence 1: Kids love his class because he always makes learning fun by using humor and interesting visual aids.

- Gives the reader an example of why he is considered a great teacher.

Body Sentence 2: His students also appreciate that Mr. Stevens never gives more than fifteen minutes of homework because he wants kids to have time to relax away from school, as long as they try their hardest during class.

- Provides another reason he's considered a great teacher.

Body Sentence 3: When it's time for tests and quizzes, he also lets kids retake anything lower than a B to boost their final grade and show they truly understand the material.

- Offers another reason students really like Mr. Stevens' class.

Conclusion Sentence: For all those reasons, Mr. Stevens is the most popular teacher in school.

- Wraps things up
- Reminds the reader what the whole purpose of the paragraph was

From "Welsh Fairy Tales"

By William Elliot Griffis

(Continued from last week's passages)

Someone may ask, why did not some brave man shoot the Afang, with a poisoned arrow, or drive a spear into him under the arms, where the flesh was tender, or cut off his head with a sharp sword?

The trouble was just here. There were plenty of brave fellows, ready to fight the monster, but nothing made of iron could pierce that hide of his. This was like armor, or one of the steel battleships of our day, and the Afang always spit out fire or poison breath down the road, up which a man was coming, long before the brave fellow could get near him. Nothing would do, but to go up into his lair, and drag him out.

But what man or company of men was strong enough to do this, when a dozen giants in a gang, with ropes as thick as a ship's hawser, could hardly tackle the job?

Nevertheless, in what neither man nor giant could do, a pretty maiden might succeed. True, she must be brave also, for how could she know, but if hungry, the Afang might eat her up?

However, one valiant damsel, of great beauty, who had lots of perfumery and plenty of pretty clothes, volunteered to bind the monster in his lair. She said, "I'm not afraid." Her sweetheart was named Gadern, and he was a young and strong hunter. He talked over the matter with her and they two resolved to act together.

Gadern went all over the country, summoning the farmers to bring their ox teams and log chains. Then he set the blacksmiths to work, forging new and especially heavy ones, made of the best native iron, from the mines, for which Wales is still famous.

Meanwhile, the lovely maiden arrayed herself in her prettiest clothes, dressed her hair in the most enticing way, hanging a white blossom on each side, over her ears, with one flower also at her neck.

When she had perfumed her garments, she sallied forth and up the lake where the big bog and the waters were and where the monster hid himself.

1. How are Gadern and the damsel both brave and important to the story in different ways?

____

____

2. How are the Afang and the maiden like opposites in this story? (You can refer back to ideas from last week's passages in your answer.)

____

____

____

____

3. What is the main purpose of Paragraph 2 in the passage?

   A. To explain why nobody had defeated the Afang yet
   B. To show how ugly and terrifying the Afang is
   C. To show what Gadern and the maiden must do to defeat the Afang
   D. To explain why people are scared of the Afang

4. What is the main purpose of Paragraph 5 in the passage?

   A. To describe the damsel who fights the Afang
   B. To explain what qualities someone needs to fight the Afang
   C. To introduce two new, important characters
   D. To show that the other people in the area are wimps for not wanting to fight the Afang

5. Based on what you've read, what do you predict is Gadern and the maiden's strategy for defeating the Afang?

____

____

____

____

____

____

Complete the Paragraph

Directions:

Each mini-paragraph below needs a sentence added to make it a strong, structured paragraph. Fill in the blanks with a sentence of your own that serves the appropriate purpose.

1. Cleaning the bathroom has to be the worst responsibility in any household. First of all, everybody knows what happens in the bathroom, and that is gross enough. To make matters worse, though, cleaning the bathroom requires a lot of different household chemicals, which can be harmful to your breathing and health, especially if you have allergies. The bathroom also contains a variety of different surfaces, from floors to sinks to toilet bowls and showers. All those areas require different cleaners and techniques, potentially turning bathroom cleaning into an all-day job. ____. (CREATE A **CONCLUSION** SENTENCE FOR THE PARAGRAPH.)

2. More and more, people are starting to rethink the way we test students in school. Increasingly, research proves that student performance on tests has very little to do with their knowledge or ability levels and more to do with confidence, comfort, and environment. For students ____.

   Teachers, however, remain divided on the issue, with some believing students should take more tests and others believing the number should go down. It's clear that, at some point in the near future, the testing system will change one way or the other. (ADD A **SUPPORTING** SENTENCE EXPLAINING HOW STUDENTS FEEL ABOUT TESTING.)

3. ____.

   Zoos provide opportunities for people to see animals that do not naturally occur in the areas where they live. For many families, that means an afternoon of fun, meeting cute animals and walking around a park. However, opponents of zoos say that those animals are harmed by living outside their native environment and shouldn't be removed from their true habitats. Those people argue that the fun people have at zoos is not worth the way the animals are treated. As you can see, the debate surrounding zoos is very complex. (CREATE A **TOPIC** SENTENCE FOR THE PARAGRAPH.)

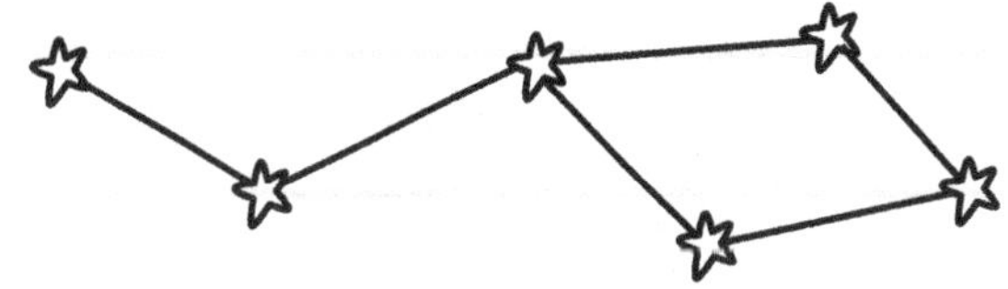

WEEK 4 DAY 1

ACTIVITIES

CLEAR, ORGANIZED PARAGRAPH STRUCTURE

FITNESS

Please be aware of your environment and be safe at all times. If you cannot do an exercise, just try your best.

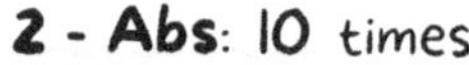

1 - Bend forward: 10 times.
Note: try to touch your feet. Make sure to keep your back straight and if needed you can bend your knees.

2 - Abs: 10 times

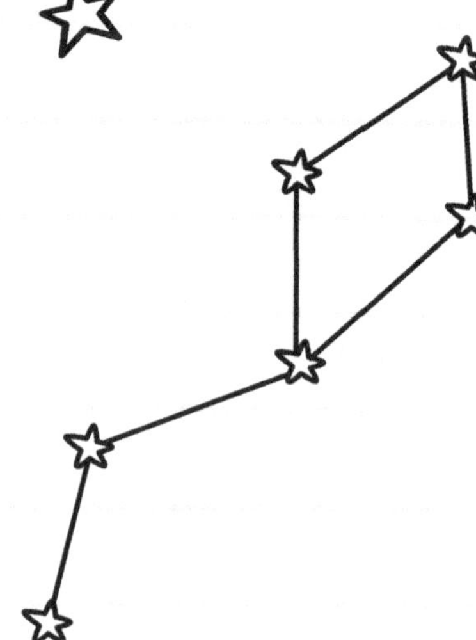

3 - Plank: 15 sec.

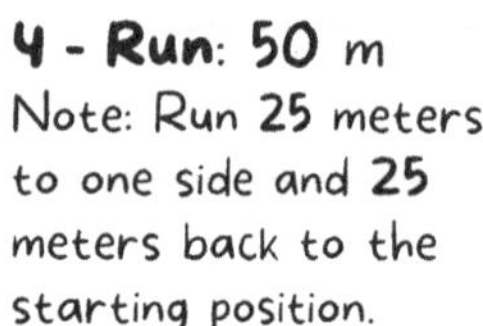

4 - Run: 50 m
Note: Run 25 meters to one side and 25 meters back to the starting position.

From "Welsh Fairy Tales"

By William Elliot Griffis

(Continued from last week's passages)

While the maiden was still quite a distance away, the terrible Afang, scenting his visitor from afar, came rushing out of his lair. When very near, he reared his head high in the air, expecting to pounce on her, with his iron clad claws and at one swallow make a breakfast of the girl.

But the odors of her perfumes were so sweet, that he forgot what he had thought to do. Moreover, when he looked at her, he was so taken with unusual beauty, that he flopped at once on his forefeet. Then he behaved just like a lovelorn beau, when his best girl comes near. He ties his necktie and pulls down his coat and brushes off the collar.

So the Afang began to spruce up. It was real fun to see how a monster behaves when smitten with love for a pretty girl. He had no idea how funny he was.

The girl was not at all afraid, but smoothed the monster's back, stroked and played with its big moustaches and tickled its neck until the Afang's throat actually gurgled with a laugh. Pretty soon he guffawed, for he was so delighted.

When he did this, the people down in the valley thought it was thunder, though the sky was clear and blue.

The maiden tickled his chin, and even put up his whiskers in curl papers. Then she stroked his neck, so that his eyes closed. Soon she had gently lulled him to slumber, by singing a cradle song, which her mother had taught her. This she did so softly, and sweetly, that in a few minutes, with its head in her lap, the monster was sound asleep and even began to snore.

Then, quietly, from their hiding places in the bushes, Gadern and his men crawled out. When near the dreaded Afang, they stood up and sneaked forward, very softly on tip toe. They had wrapped the links of the chain in grass and leaves, so that no clanking was heard. They also held the oxen's yokes, so that nobody or anything could rattle, or make any noise. Slowly but surely they passed the chain over its body, in the middle, besides binding the brute securely between its fore and hind legs.

All this time, the monster slept on, for the girl kept on crooning her melody.

READING PASSAGE
CLEAR, ORGANIZED PARAGRAPH STRUCTURE

1. How did Gadern and the maiden's strategy compare to the prediction you made at the end of Day 1?

____

____

2. How is the description of the Afang's actions in this passage different from the descriptions of Afang that we've seen in previous passages?

____

____

3. Which transition word could be added at the beginning of Paragraph 4?

   A. Consequently
   B. However
   C. Conversely
   D. Furthermore

4. Which transition word could be used instead of "Then" at the beginning of Paragraph 7?

   A. Ultimately
   B. However
   C. Conversely
   D. Next

5. How does this story show that you don't have to fight in the traditional way to be a hero?

____

____

____

____

____

____

Choosing the Order of Sentences

Directions:

Each question below lists five sentences belonging to a paragraph. Read all the sentences carefully, then, on the lines below, use the corresponding letter to communicate which order the sentences should go in. Be sure to read the sentences out loud in the order you're recommending to make sure they sound correct.

1.

A. Warm the pan over medium heat and add a thin layer of butter to one side of the tortilla.

B. Place the tortilla, butter side down in the pan, put a layer of cheese over half the tortilla, and then fold it closed.

C. All you need to get started is a tortilla, some shredded cheese, a little butter, and a pan.

D. Making a quesadilla at home is fun and easy.

E. Cook your quesadilla for a few minutes on both sides, and it's ready to go!

ORDER OF SENTENCES:

TOPIC SENTENCE: ________

SUPPORT 1: ________

SUPPORT 2: ________

SUPPORT 3: ________

CONCLUSION: ________

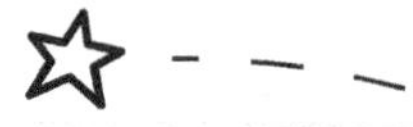

2.

A. If the next game is half as exciting, we're in for a wild ride.

B. Last night's baseball game was absolutely thrilling.

C. The home team ultimately won on a walk-off home run with the bases loaded and two outs.

D. First of all, it was a playoff game, so the stakes were high.

E. Both starting pitchers did well, and the score was tight into the late innings.

ORDER OF SENTENCES:

TOPIC SENTENCE: ________

SUPPORT 1: ________

SUPPORT 2: ________

SUPPORT 3: ________

CONCLUSION: ________

FITNESS

Please be aware of your environment and be safe at all times. If you cannot do an exercise, just try your best.

Repeat these exercises **3 ROUNDS**

1 - Squats: 15 times. Note: imagine you are trying to sit on a chair.

2 - Side Bending: 10 times to each side. Note: try to touch your feet.

3 - Tree Pose: Stay as long as possible. Note: do the same with the other leg.

  **MATH**

Numerical Expressions

1. What is 124 - (6 x 9) + 12?

   A. 76
   B. 82
   C. 88
   D. 94

2. Solve the problem (52 + 14) x 8 - 14.

   A. 416
   B. 498
   C. 514
   D. 525

3. Which number sentence is equals to 143?

   A. 98 + (7 x 9)
   B. (23 + 32) x 5
   C. (65 - 11) ÷ 3 + 127
   D. 265 + (3 x 12) - 158

4. Which number sentence below is true?

   A. 456 - (24 x 12) = 158
   B. (208 ÷ 8) + 44 = 70
   C. 18 + (20 x 14) - 65 = 243
   D. (28 x 13) + 72 - 96 = 338

5. Solve the problem using the **order of operations, PEMDAS.**

   132 + 184 ÷ 8 - 56

   Answer ____________________

6. What is the first expression you need to evaluate in the problem?
   145 - 65 x 3.

   Answer ____________________

7. What is 65 ÷ 5 + 28 - 7?

   A. 34
   B. 36
   C. 43
   D. 51

8. Evaluate the expression
   (67 + 15) x 2 - 144.

   A. 15
   B. 20
   C. 25
   D. 30

9. Choose the number that fits the blank for the problem below.

   25 x 4 + 36 - ____ = 90

   A. 36
   B. 42
   C. 46
   D. 49

10. Solve the problem 68 - (162 ÷ 6 + 20).

    A. 34
    B. 18
    C. 27
    D. 21

11. Complete the problem below.

    (46 - 39) x ____ + 54 = 138

    Answer ____________________

12. What is the first expression you need to evaluate in the problem?
    46 x (12 + 26) - 12.

    Answer ____________________

  MATH

Tables/Charts and understanding data

The table below shows the hours Sean worked each month during summer. Use the table to answer questions 1 - 2

Months	Working hours
June	48
July	56
August	52

1. Which month did he work the most?

   Answer ____________________

2. From June to July did the number of hours he worked increase or decrease?

   Answer ____________________

   ____

The table below shows the amount of ice cream sold at the park. Use the data to answer questions 3 - 5.

Days	Sold Ice Cream
Monday	112
Tuesday	145
Wednesday	136
Thursday	124
Friday	156
Saturday	186

3. Which day had the least ice cream sold?

   Answer ____________________

4. How many ice creams were sold on Tuesday?

   Answer ____________________

5. What is the difference in the number of ice creams sold on Thursday and the number of ice creams sold on Friday?

   A. 33
   B. 32
   C. 34
   D. 36

FITNESS

Please be aware of your environment and be safe at all times. If you cannot do an exercise, just try your best.

Repeat these exercises **3 ROUNDS**

1 - Bend forward: 10 times.
Note: try to touch your feet. Make sure to keep your back straight and if needed you can bend your knees.

2 - Lunges: 5 times to each leg.
Note: Use your body weight or books as weight to do leg lunges.

3 - Plank: 15 sec.

4 - Abs: 10 times

WEEK 4 DAY 4  MATH

Tables/Charts and understanding data

The table below shows the number of mice caught by a cat in a week. Use the data to answer questions 1 - 3.

Days	Mice Caught
Monday	0
Tuesday	3
Wednesday	1
Thursday	5
Friday	2
Saturday	2

1. What is the total number of mice caught?

   Answer ____________________

2. Were fewer mice caught on Tuesday or on Thursday?

   Answer ____________________

3. Were there at least 4 caught mice on Wednesday and Friday?

   Answer ____________________

The chart below shows the number of essays a class wrote each month. Use the data to answer questions 4 - 5.

Month	Number of essays
September	56
October	84
November	73
December	92

4. Which month shows the fewest amount of essays written by the class?

   A. September
   B. October
   C. November
   D. December

5. Were more essays written in October or in December?

   Answer ____________________

Bar graph & Line graph

The bar graph below shows the number of books sold a week. Use the data to answer questions 1 - 3.

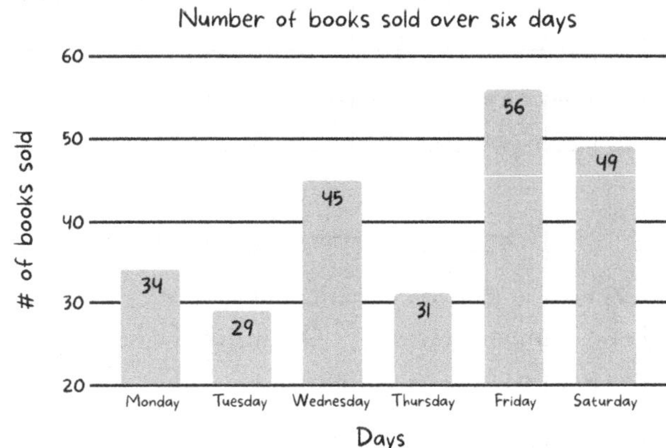

1. Which day were the most books sold?

   Answer ____________________

2. From Wednesday to Thursday did the amount of books sold increase or decrease? By how much?

   Answer ____________________

3. On Saturday the goal was to sell at least 45 books. Was that goal reached? Explain your reasoning.

   Answer ____________________

WEEK 4 DAY 4 MATH

David tracked the temperature outdoor for a day. Use the data to answer questions 4 - 6.

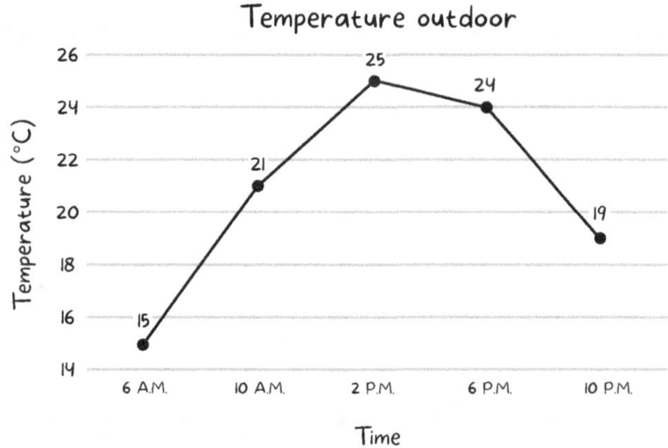

4. What time was the highest temperature?

   Answer ____________________

5. From 6 pm. to 10 pm. did the temperature increase or decrease? Explain your reasoning.

   Answer ____________________

6. What is the difference between the temperature at 10 am. and the temperature at 10 pm.?

   Answer ____________________

A confectionery company asked its customers which sweets were their favorite. They recorded the results in the bar graph below. Use the data to answer questions 7 - 8.

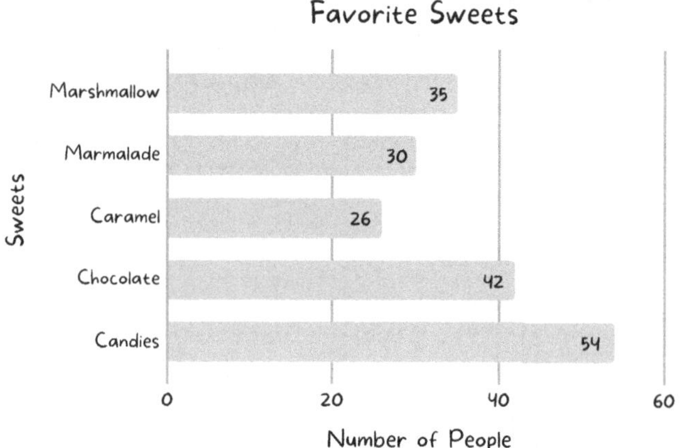

7. What is the combined number of people who liked marshmallow and marmalade?

   A. 56
   B. 65
   C. 68
   D. 96

8. How many fewer people liked caramel than those who liked candies?

   Answer ____________________

FITNESS

Please be aware of your environment and be safe at all times. If you cannot do an exercise, just try your best.

Repeat these exercises **3 ROUNDS**

1 - High Plank: 15 sec.

2 - Abs: 10 times

3 - Side Bending: 10 times to each side. Note: try to touch your feet.

WEEK 4 DAY 5  MATH

Line of symmetry

1. How many lines of symmetry does this shape have?

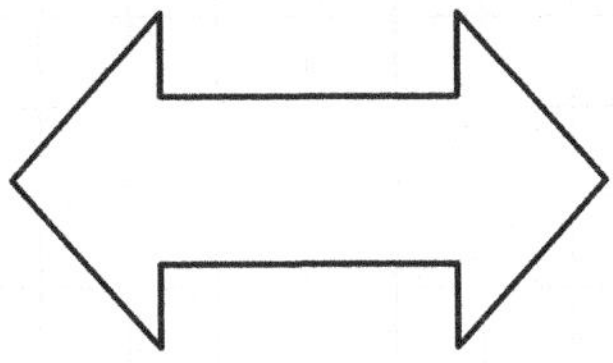

A. 1
B. 2
C. 3
D. 4

2. In the shape below, which of the following is NOT a line of symmetry?

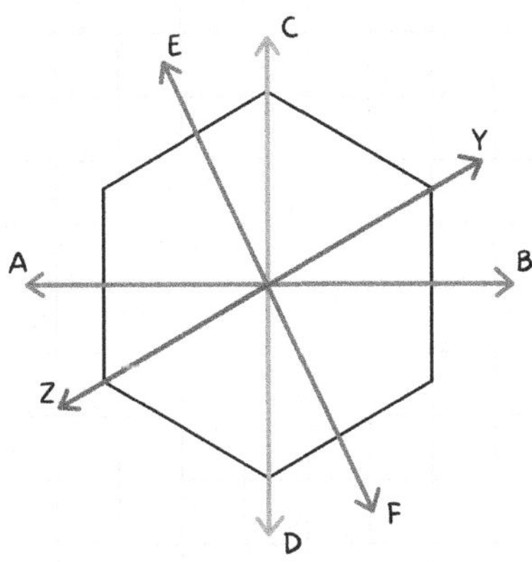

A. AB
B. CD
C. EF
D. ZY

3. Which of the following diagrams has the correct line of symmetry?

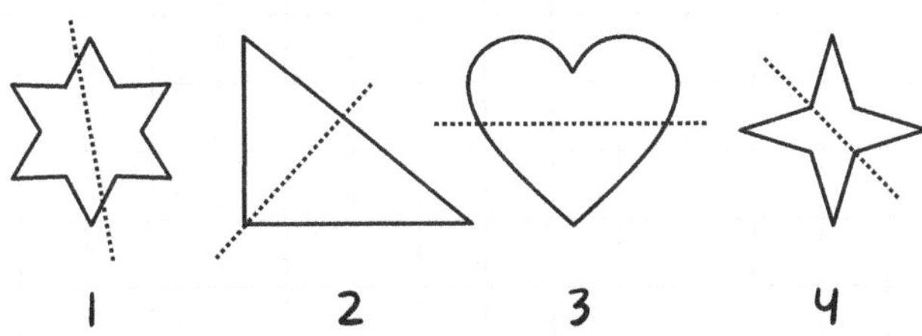

A. 1
B. 2
C. 3
D. 4

4. Which shape appears to have exactly 1 line of symmetry?

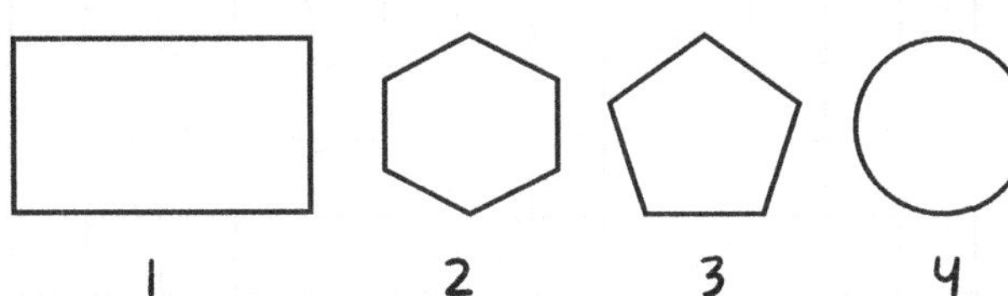

A. 1
B. 2
C. 3
D. 4

5. Which shape appears to have zero lines of symmetry?

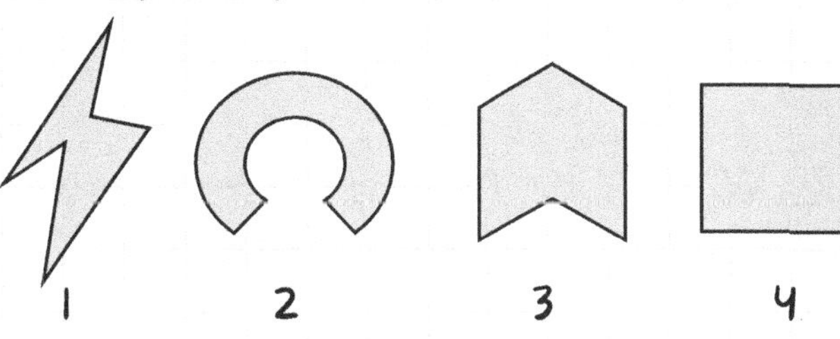

A. 1
B. 2
C. 3
D. 4

6. Is the shape below symmetrical?

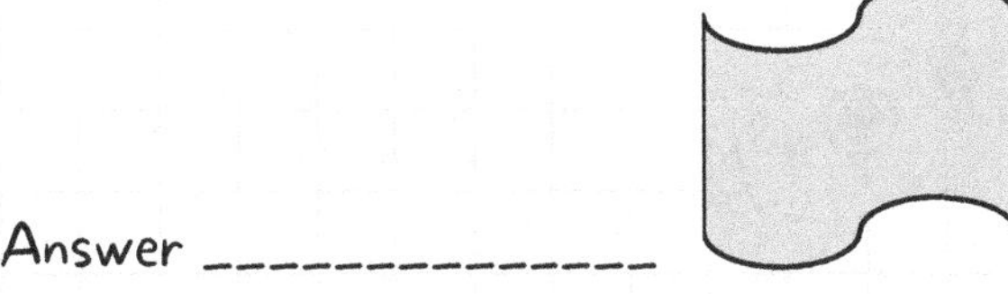

Answer _____________

7. How many lines of symmetry does this shape have?

Answer _____________

WEEK 4 DAY 5  MATH

Identifying perpendicular lines, parallel lines, points, lines and rays.

Use the drawing below to answer questions 1 - 2.

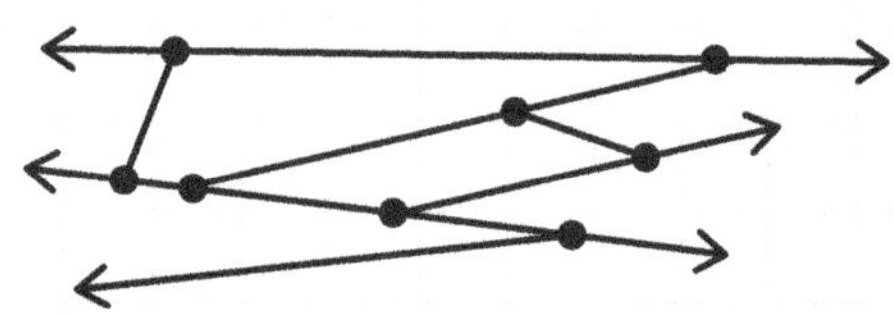

1. How many lines are in the drawing?

   A. 1
   B. 2
   C. 3
   D. 4

2. Which of the following statements most accurately describes a line segment?

   A. A line segment extends continuously in both directions.
   B. A line segment is always perpendicular to a ray.
   C. A line segment is a part of a line and has two end points.
   D. None of the above

Use the drawing below to answer questions 3 - 4.

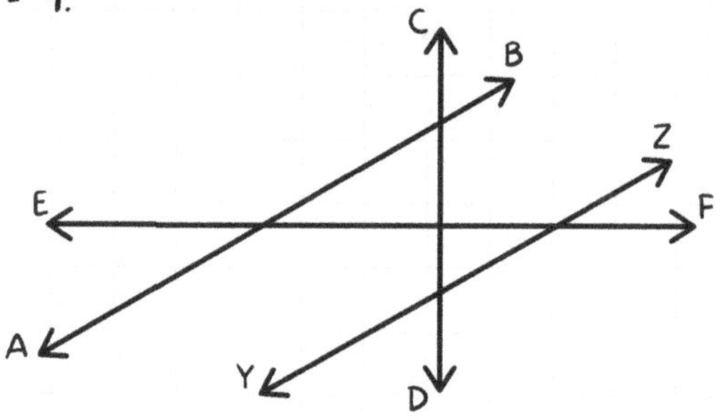

3. Which lines are parallel?

   A. AB and CD
   B. CD and EF
   C. CD and YZ
   D. AB and YZ

4. Which lines are perpendicular?

   A. AB and CD
   B. CD and EF
   C. EF and YZ
   D. CD and YZ

YOGA

Please be aware of your environment and be safe at all times. If you cannot do an exercise, just try your best.

START

1 - Bend Down: 20 sec.

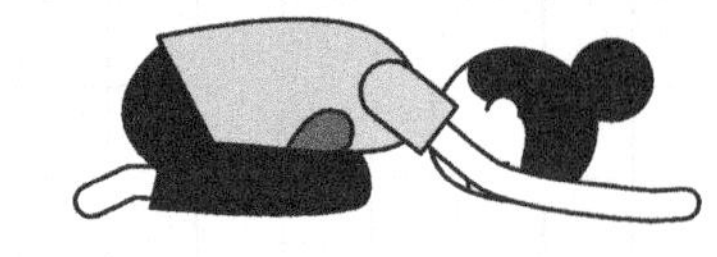

2 - Child Pose: 20 sec.

3 - Chair: 20 sec.

4 -Book Pose: 20 sec. Note: Keep your core tight. Legs shoud be across your eyes.

5 - Shavasana: as long as you can. Note: think of happy moments and relax your mind.

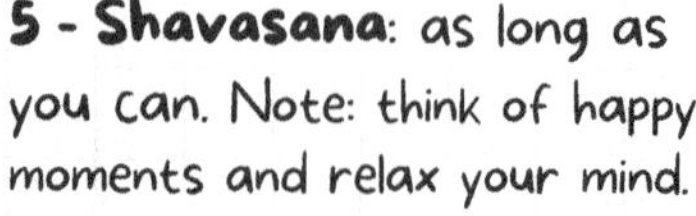

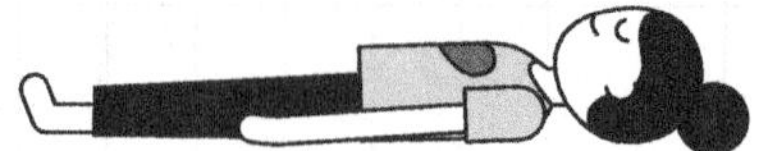

WEEK 4 DAY 6 EXPERIMENT

Describing Properties

Based on our work so far this summer, we know that all objects are made of **matter**, and that matter is made up of **atoms** and **molecules**, which we can't see. However, all matter also has **properties**. Basically, that means that every object has certain characteristics that we can observe. For example, a person has a height, a weight, a hair color, a fashion sense, an eye color, etc. All of those are **properties**. Part of the scientific mindset is being able to think about objects in terms of their **properties**.

Materials:

- An assortment of various household objects (at least 10) of different sizes, shapes, colors, etc. (nothing bigger than a basketball)
- A scale that can measure in grams or ounces (a kitchen scale is ideal)
- A ruler or flexible tape measure
- Notepaper

Procedure:

1. Using your ruler and notepaper, make a chart or table that has at least 10 rows (one for each object you gathered) and 6 columns.
2. Label the first column Object, and then write the names of the different objects you chose below it.
3. Label each of your 5 columns in this order: **Shape, Color, Weight, Dimensions, Materials.** It should look like this:

OBJECT	SHAPE	COLOR	WEIGHT	DIMENSIONS	MATERIALS
Baseball					
Nickel					
Saucer					
Etc.					

4. Take your objects one at a time, and use your ruler, tape measure, scale, and other tools to complete the chart for each one. If one of your objects is more than one color, just write down all the colors in it. For dimensions, try to get a general sense of how many inches big something is. If it's rectangular, measure its length and width. If it's round, try to figure out how big around it is. For "Materials" write down what the object appears to be made out of (leather, rubber, paper, aluminum, etc.).

WEEK 4 DAY 6  EXPERIMENT

Follow-Up Question:

1. If you were going to add two more columns (property categories) to the table, which ones would you add and why?

2. What's an example of two objects that appear similar at first, but actually have very different properties?

YOGA

Please be aware of your environment and be safe at all times. If you cannot do an exercise, just try your best.

2 - Down Dog: 20 sec.

3 - Stretching: Stay as long as possible.
Note: do on one leg then on another.

4 - Lower Plank: 20 sec.
Note: Keep your back straight and body tight.

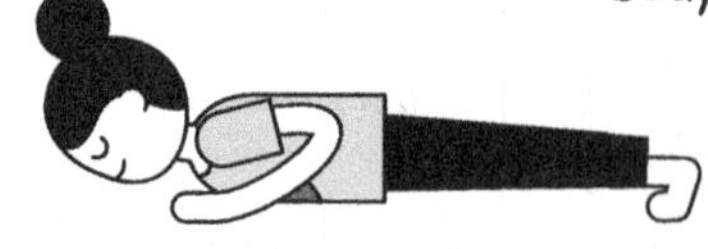

1 - Tree Pose: Stay as long as possible.
Note: do on one leg then on another.

START

6 - Shavasana: 10 min.
Note: this pose is very important and provides you with long term benefits. Try not to skip this. Close your eyes and imagine who you want to be and what your goals are! Always think happy thoughts.

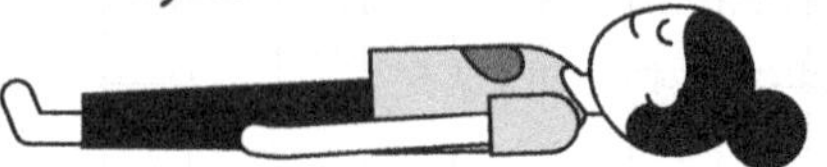

5 - Book Pose: 20 sec.
Note: Keep your core tight. Legs should be across from your eyes.

WEEK 4 DAY 7  MAZE

Task: Connect the planets and the spaceships.

A B 1 2 C 3 4 5 E D

Planet 1	Spaceship ___
Planet 2	Spaceship ___
Planet 3	Spaceship ___
Planet 4	Spaceship ___
Planet 5	Spaceship ___

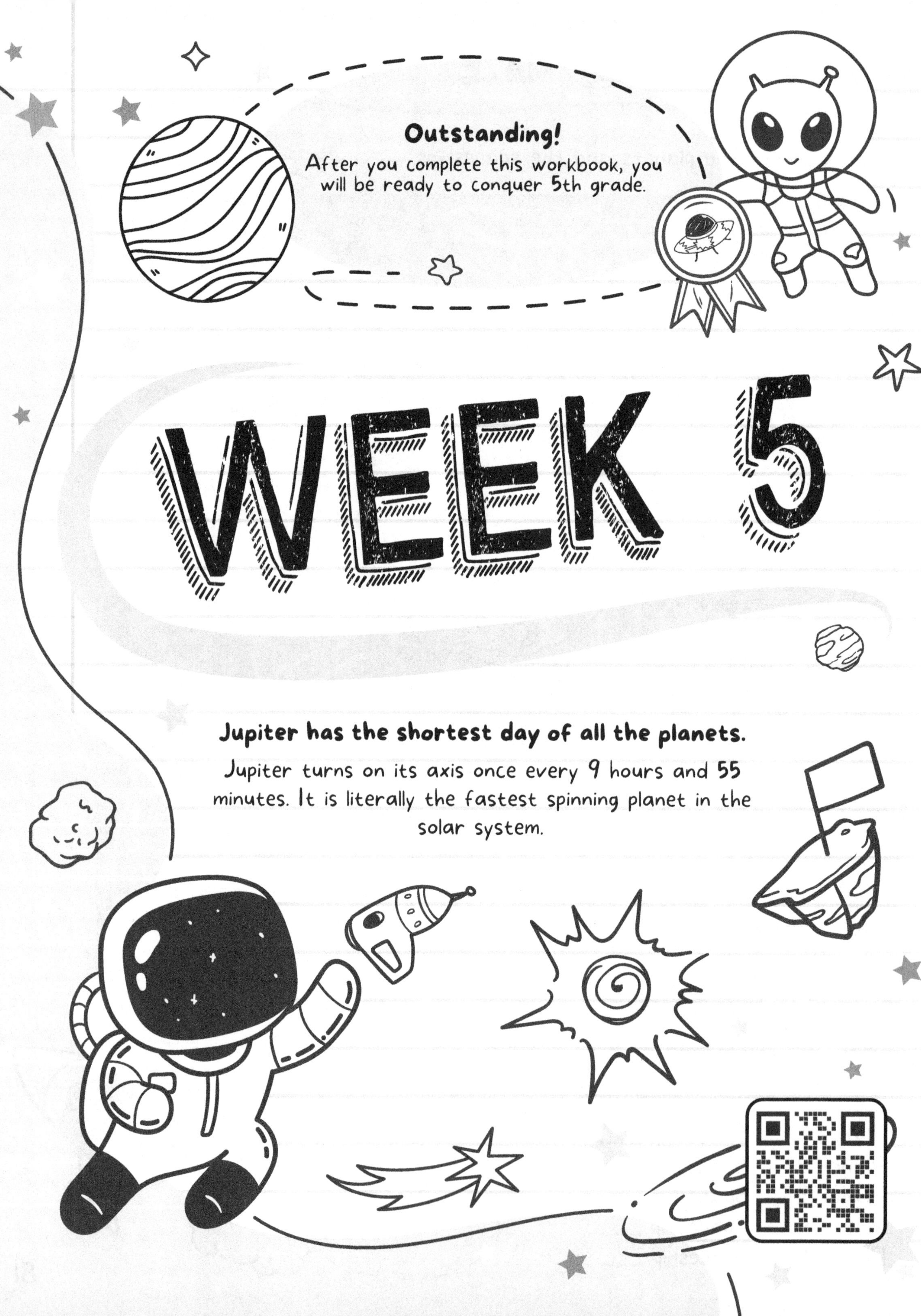

Outstanding!
After you complete this workbook, you will be ready to conquer 5th grade.
WEEK 5
Jupiter has the shortest day of all the planets.
Jupiter turns on its axis once every 9 hours and 55 minutes. It is literally the fastest spinning planet in the solar system.

WEEK 5 DAY 1

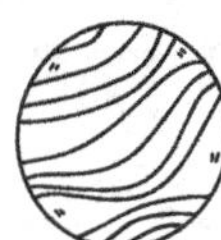

OVERVIEW OF ENGLISH CONCEPTS
1ST, 2ND AND 3RD PERSON PRONOUNS

As you've probably noticed from your own reading, not all ideas are communicated in the same way. Depending on what kind of writing they're doing, and how they want to interact with the audience, authors can write things in either **first person, second person, or third person**. **First person** is a voice that uses "I" and communicates information to the audience in a personal way. **Second person** directly addresses the audience as "you" and is useful for giving directions or communicating information that people need to act on. **Third person** does not address the author or speaker directly, but instead presents information in an impersonal, factual way.

One of the best ways to identify which **person** something is written in is by assessing the **pronouns** being used. Pronouns are those short words (like "I", "he", or "them") that are used to replace longer nouns in sentences.

Key Terms

First Person: Written from the perspective of someone telling a story from personal experience (using "I", "me", "us", and "we")

Second Person: Directly addressing the audience using the word "you"

Third Person: Written from an outside perspective of someone telling a story they were not personally involved in (using "he/him", "she/her", "it", "they", and "them").

Pronouns: Shorter words used to replace **nouns** (people, places, or things) to provide a quicker, smoother reading experience

1st, 2nd, and 3rd Person Pronouns

Person	Singular Pronouns	Plural Pronouns
FIRST PERSON	I, me	We, us
SECOND PERSON	You	You, "You all"
THIRD PERSON	He/Him (for males), She/Her (for females), It (for objects, animals, and ideas)	Them/Them

Hints:

- If you have a **narrator** or **author** who uses "I" in the story at all, it's **first person.**
- If something is a set of directions, orders, or instructions, it's probably written in **second person.**
- If a story has a narrator who just describes the scene without ever discussing their own involvement in the story, it's probably written in **third person.**

From King Arthur's Knights

By Henry Gilbert

On Christmas Eve the city throbbed with the clank of arms and the tramp of the great retinues of princes, kings and powerful lords who had come at the archbishop's summons, and by day and night the narrow ways were crowded with armed men. Long ere the dawn of Christmas Day, the lords and the common people betook themselves along the wide road which led across to the church, which then stood in a wide space amid fields, and all knelt therein to mass.

While it was yet dark a great strange cry rang out in the churchyard. Some ran forth, and there by the wall behind the high altar they saw a vast stone, four-square, that had not been there before, and in the middle thereof was stuck a great wedge of steel, and sticking therefrom by the point was a rich sword. On the blade were written words in Latin, which a clerk read forth, which said, "Whoso pulleth this sword out of this stone and wedge of steel is rightwise born King of all Britain."

The clerk ran into the church and told the archbishop, and men were all amazed and would have gone instantly to see this marvel, but the archbishop bade them stay.

"Finish your prayers to God," he said, "for no man may touch this strange thing till high mass be done."

When mass was finished, all poured forth from the church and thronged about the stone, and marvelled at the words on the sword. First King Lot, with a light laugh, took hold of the handle and essayed to pull out the point of the sword, but he could not, and his face went hot and angry. Then King Nentres of Garlot took his place with a jest, but though he heaved at the sword with all his burly strength, till it seemed like to snap, he could not move it, and so let go at last with an angry oath. All the others essayed in like manner, but by none was it moved a jot, and all stood about discomfited, looking with black looks at one another and the stone.

"He that is rightwise born ruler of Britain is not here," said the archbishop at length, "but doubt not he shall come in God's good time. Meanwhile, let a tent be raised over the stone, and do ye lords appoint ten of your number to watch over it, and we will essay the sword again after New Year's Day.

WEEK 5 DAY 1

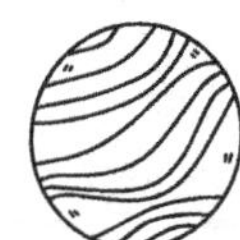

READING PASSAGE
1ST, 2ND AND 3RD PERSON PRONOUNS

1. Based on the passage, what are **three** unusual or special things about the sword that is described?

____

____

2. Why are all the knights and kings in Paragraph 5 frustrated?

____

____

____

____

3. Which kind of **pronouns** do not occur in this passage?

   A. First Person
   B. Second Person
   C. Third Person
   D. All three kinds of pronouns are used at least once

4. Based on context clues, which of these is the best definition for **"essayed"** in Paragraph 5?

   A. Wrote an essay
   B. Fell
   C. Attempted
   D. Succeeded

5. In your own words, describe the plan that the characters make at the end of this passage.

____

____

____

____

____

____

Identifying First, Second, and Third Person Pronouns

Directions:

Read each sentence, then circle all the personal pronouns and write a **"1", "2", or "3"** above each one to indicate whether it is a first, second, or third person pronoun. **NOTE:** There may be more than one personal pronoun in each sentence!

1. Ms. Variano is a great teacher because she always makes sure we understand things before she moves on to the next idea.
2. You need to clean things up in here before I'm going to let you go over to Mike's house to play.
3. Otto and Christine are close friends, but she can get very competitive when they play sports against each other.
4. Mom says I can't play football because it is too rough, and she doesn't want me to get hurt.
5. The squirrel scurried under the fence and up a tree when it saw the family dog emerge from the house.

Please be aware of your environment and be safe at all times. If you cannot do an exercise, just try your best.

Repeat these exercises **3 ROUNDS**

3 - Plank: 15 sec.

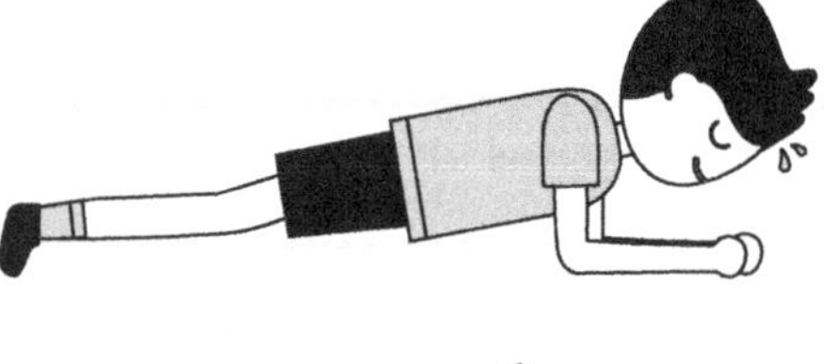

2 - Abs: 10 times

4 - Run: 50m
Note: Run 25 meters to one side and 25 meters back to the starting position.

1 - Bend forward: 10 times.
Note: try to touch your feet. Make sure to keep your back straight and if needed you can bend your knees.

From King Arthur's Knights

By Henry Gilbert

(Continued from Day 1's Passage)

So that the kings and lords should be kept together, the archbishop appointed a great tournament to be held on New Year's Day on the waste land north of the city, which men now call Smithfield.

Now when the day was come, a certain lord, Sir Ector de Morven, who had great lands about the isle of Thorney, rode towards the jousts with his son, Sir Kay, and young Arthur, who was Sir Kay's foster-brother. When they had got nearly to the place, suddenly Sir Kay bethought him that he had left his sword at home.

"Do you ride back, young Arthur," he said, "and fetch me my sword, for if I do not have it I may not fight."

Willingly Arthur turned his horse and rode back swiftly. But when he had arrived at the house, he found it shut up and none was within, for all had gone to the jousts. Then was he a little wroth, and rode back wondering how he should obtain a sword for his foster-brother.

Suddenly, as he saw the tower of St. Paul's church through the trees, he bethought him of the sword in the stone, about which many men had spoken in his hearing.

"I will ride thither," said he, "and see if I may get that sword for my brother, for he shall not be without a sword this day."

When he came to the churchyard, he tied his horse to the stile, and went through the grave-mounds to the tent wherein was the sword. He found the place unwatched, and the flashing sword was sticking by the point in the stone.

Lightly he grasped the handle of the sword with one hand, and it came forth straightway!

1. Based on the passage, how would you describe **Arthur's** personality?

___

___

2. Based on what you read on Day 1, why are the events of this passage surprising or unexpected?

___

___

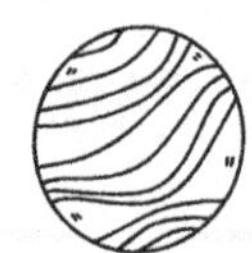

3. Which kinds of pronoun are used in the sentence, "Do you ride back, young Arthur... and fetch me my sword" (Paragraph 3)?

   A. First and Second Person
   B. First and Third Person
   C. Second and Third Person
   D. First, Second, and Third Person

4. Based on context, what can we assume the word **"thither"** means, as it is used in Paragraph 5?

   A. Their
   B. Over there
   C. Further
   D. Feather

5. Based on this passage and the one from Day 1, what do you predict will happen next in the story? What details make you think that way?

____

____

____

____

____

____

Identifying Pronoun Antecedents

Directions:

Read each sentence, then circle all the personal pronouns and, for each one, draw an arrow that points at that pronoun's **antecedent** (the person, place, or thing it's referring to). **NOTE:** You do not need to find an antecedent for "I" or "me."

1. The cat stalked across the lawn until it got close enough to the chipmunk to attempt to pounce on it.

2. When parents are too strict with children, they run the risk of creating an environment where kids don't believe they are free to express concerns.

3. I love that lamp because it was a gift from Aunt Suzie, and she was my favorite family member growing up.

4. Most scientists agree that the Tasmanian Tiger is extinct, but some of them believe it still lives in isolated areas.

5. A lot of people say Mark has bad luck, but they don't want to admit the real problem, which is that he is lazy.

Please be aware of your environment and be safe at all times. If you cannot do an exercise, just try your best.

Repeat these exercises **3 ROUNDS**

1 - Squats: 15 times. Note: imagine you are trying to sit on a chair.

2 - Side Bending: 10 times to each side. Note: try to touch your feet.

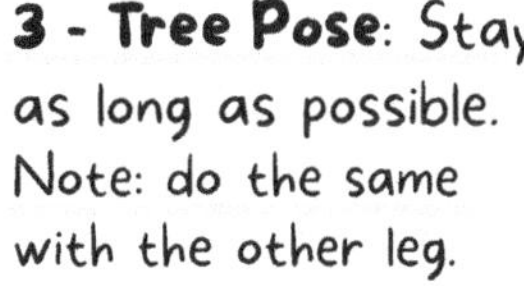

3 - Tree Pose: Stay as long as possible. Note: do the same with the other leg.

Time

1. What is 8 hours added to 326 minutes?

   A. 12 hours 46 minutes
   B. 13 hours 16 minutes
   C. 13 hours 26 minutes
   D. 13 hours 36 minutes

2. The movie started at 5:30 p.m. and ended at 7:50 p.m. How much time passed?

   A. 1 hour 50 minutes
   B. 2 hours 20 minutes
   C. 2 hours 30 minutes
   D. 2 hours 50 minutes

3. Find 36 hours subtracted from 3 days.

   A. 2 days 4 hours
   B. 1 day 5 hours
   C. 1 day 14 hours
   D. 1 day 12 hours

4. Two days is what fraction of a week?

   A. $\frac{1}{7}$
   B. $\frac{2}{7}$
   C. 0.2
   D. $\frac{2}{5}$

5. Which clock shows the starting time for this problem?

   _____ + 3 hours and 25 minutes = 4:50

1 2 3 4

Answer ______________________

6. What time will it be in three hours and seventeen minutes?

   A. 10:15
   B. 10:17
   C. 10:25
   D. 10:27

7. Six hours is what fraction of a day?

   A. $\frac{1}{2}$
   B. $\frac{1}{4}$
   C. $\frac{6}{12}$
   D. $\frac{3}{4}$

8. If it is currently 6:35pm, what time will it be in 2 hours and 44 minutes?

   Answer ______________________

9. What is the elapsed time between 3:47 pm and 8:24 pm?

   Answer ______________________

10. How minutes are in $\frac{4}{12}$ of an hour?

    Answer ______________________

Unit conversions (minutes, seconds, hours, liters, etc)

1. How many seconds are in 12 minutes?

   A. 600 seconds
   B. 660 seconds
   C. 720 seconds
   D. 760 seconds

WEEK 5 DAY 3  MATH

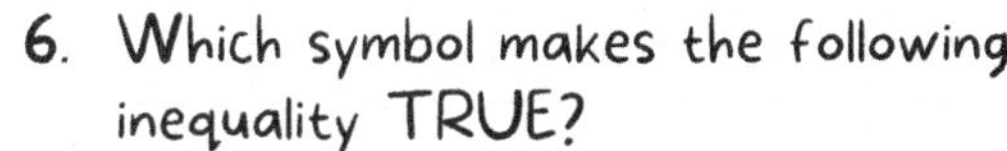

2. Determine what number makes the conversion true.

   ____ hours = 9 days

   A. 184
   B. 216
   C. 235
   D. 246

3. How many inches are in 14 feet?

   A. 168 inches
   B. 188 inches
   C. 206 inches
   D. 214 inches

4. If a flour package weighs about 0.6 kilograms, how many grams does the flour package weigh?

   A. 60 grams
   B. 660 grams
   C. 600 grams
   D. 6,000 grams

5. How many quarts are in 23 gallons?

   A. 82 qt
   B. 92 qt
   C. 96 qt
   D. 112 qt

6. Which symbol makes the following inequality TRUE?

   567 minutes ____ 9 hours

   A. >
   B. <
   C. =
   D. +

7. Determine what number makes the conversion true.

   ____ pounds = 240 ounce

   A. 12
   B. 14
   C. 15
   D. 20

8. What is 350 grams expressed in kilograms?

   Answer ____________________

9. How many meters are in 0.8 kilometers?

   Answer ____________________

FITNESS ☆

Please be aware of your environment and be safe at all times. If you cannot do an exercise, just try your best.

Repeat these exercises **3 ROUNDS**

1 - Bend forward: 10 times.
Note: try to touch your feet. Make sure to keep your back straight and if needed you can bend your knees.

2 - Lunges: 5 times to each leg.
Note: Use your body weight or books as weight to do leg lunges.

3 - Plank: 15 sec.

4 - Abs: 10 times

Word problems for unit conversions

1. Mrs. Howard bought $2\frac{1}{2}$ gallons of milk. How much milk did she buy in pints?

   A. 16 pints
   B. 20 pints
   C. 22 pints
   D. 24 pints

2. Ellie started cleaning her room at 9:25. She spent 85 minutes completing the job. What time did she finish?

   A. 10:25
   B. 10:45
   C. 10:50
   D. 11:05

3. Ethan has four packages of nuts. Each package weighs 500 grams. How many **kilograms** of nuts does Ethan have?

   A. 1 kg
   B. 2 kg
   C. 3 kg
   D. 4 kg

4. Tina ran 890 yards on Tuesday and 930 yards on Wednesday. How many miles did she run in total? Note: 1,760 yards = 1 mile

   A. 1 mi 20 yd
   B. 1 mi 30 yd
   C. 1 mi 50 yd
   D. 1 mi 60 yd

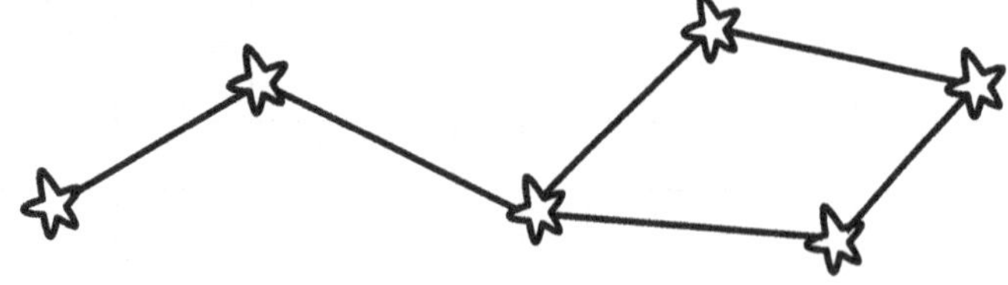

5. The electrical cable to supply new buildings with electricity will be 6 km long. There is already 0.800 km of electrical cable put on one side and 31,700 cm from the other side. How many meters of electrical cable still need to be installed?

   A. 4,883 m
   B. 4,888 m
   C. 4,943 m
   D. 4,969 m

6. In September, Teddy spent 156 hours studying. In October, he spent 6 days studying. What is the combined length of time in hours he spent studying?

   Answer ______________________

7. Water from a barrel was put into 25 bottles, each bottle holding 700 milliliters of water. If we use bottles that can each hold 0.5 liters of water, how many bottles do we need to hold the same amount of water from the barrel?

   A. 27 bottles
   B. 35 bottles
   C. 39 bottles
   D. 42 bottles

8. Mellisa rode 2 kilometers on her bike. Jack rode 3,000 meters on his bike. Who rode the farthest and how much farther did they ride? (Write your answer in km.)

   Answer ______________________

9. A certain farm received a delivery order for a supermarket. The order was 8,000 ml of whole milk charged at $4 per liter, 11 liters of butter milk charged at $5 per liter, and 7,000 milliliters of skim milk charged at $3 per liter. What is the total cost for this order?

   A. $96
   B. $102
   C. $108
   D. $116

10. A large box of candies weighed $8\frac{1}{4}$ pounds. A small box of nails weighed 63 ounces. What is the total amount of weight of these two boxes in **ounces**?

    Answer ____________________

Word problems dealing with mass and volume

1. For Halloween, Mark received $8\frac{3}{4}$ pounds of sweets. After two weeks his family had eaten $5\frac{1}{4}$ pounds of the sweets. How many pounds of sweets does he have left?

   Answer ____________________

2. A chef used 118 ounces of chicken to make lunch for the entire restaurant. For dinner he used twice as many ounces of chicken. How many ounces of chicken did he use in total?

   Answer ____________________

3. For a birthday party, Harper bought 14 pints of orange juice and 4 bottles of sodas that each had a volume of 2 pints. How many pints of drinks did she buy in total?

   A. 20 pt
   B. 22 pt
   C. 24 pt
   D. 26 pt

4. A large container could hold 485 cups of water. There are also sixteen smaller containers that could hold 85 cups each. How many cups in total can all the containers hold?

   A. 1,845
   B. 1,935
   C. 2.115
   D. 2,265

FITNESS 

Please be aware of your environment and be safe at all times. If you cannot do an exercise, just try your best.

Repeat these exercises **3 ROUNDS**

1 - High Plank: 15 sec.

2 - Abs: 10 times

3 - Side Bending: 10 times to each side. Note: try to touch your feet.

Word problems dealing with mass and volume

1. A big bag weighed 62 kilograms. A small bag weighed 13 kilograms. If you had two big bags and 9 small bags, how much would they weigh all together?

   A. 168 kg
   B. 196 kg
   C. 241 kg
   D. 256 kg

2. Aiden bought a box of candied fruit that weighed $5\frac{3}{4}$ kilograms. If he bought a second box that weighed $4\frac{2}{4}$ kilograms, what is the combined weight of both boxes?

   Answer ____________________

3. Whitney has 9 friends. She has 243 ounces of nuts which she wants to share with her friends equally. How many ounces of nuts will each friend get?

   A. 25 oz
   B. 27 oz
   C. 32 oz
   D. 36 oz

4. Valery had $9\frac{1}{6}$ cups of flour. If she used $4\frac{4}{6}$ cups for baking pancakes, how many cups of flour did she have left?

   A. $3\frac{5}{6}$
   B. $4\frac{1}{6}$
   C. $4\frac{2}{6}$
   D. $4\frac{3}{6}$

5. An orchard owner was counting the number of boxes with apples he had in total. Each of his 29 boxes had 25 kilograms of apples in it. How many kilograms of apples did he have in total?

   Answer ____________________

6. A baker had 20 boxes of sweets. He split 9,300 grams of sweets evenly between the boxes. How many grams of sweets are in each box?

   Answer ____________________

Temperature (Celsius)

1. Which thermometer represents the temperature 26°?

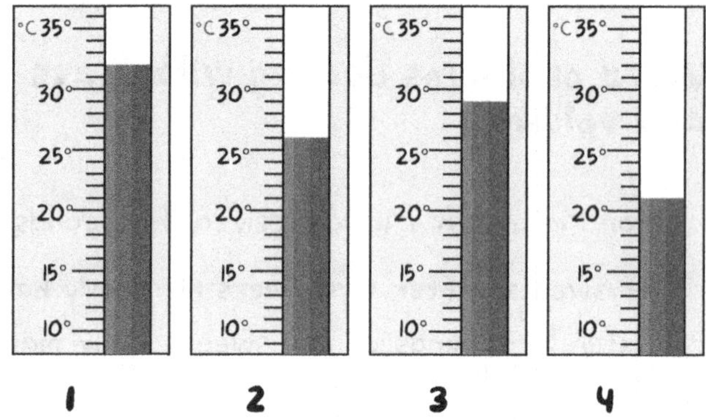

   A. 1
   B. 2
   C. 3
   D. 4

2. Determine the difference between temperatures for the following thermometers.

   A. 6°C
   B. 8°C
   C. 10°C
   D. 12°C

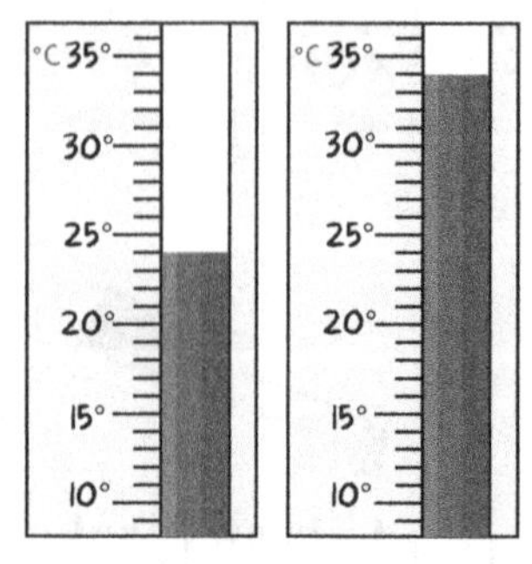

WEEK 5 DAY 5  MATH

3. The temperature outside was 37° Celsius. During the next few hours it decreased by 13° and then increased by 14°. What is the new temperature?

    A. 10°C
    B. 13°C
    C. 34°C
    D. 38°C

4. Which thermometer represents the temperature 11°?

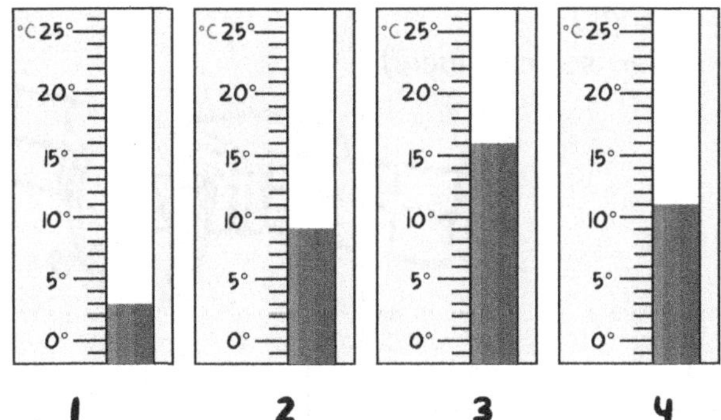

1 2 3 4

    A. 1
    B. 2
    C. 3
    D. 4

5. The thermometer showed 2°C in the morning. Then, the temperature increased by 3°C and then decreased by 1°C and then increased by 4°C. What is the current temperature the thermometer shows?

    A. 3°C
    B. 6°C
    C. 8°C
    D. 10°C

6. What is the difference between the measurements on the first and the second thermometer?

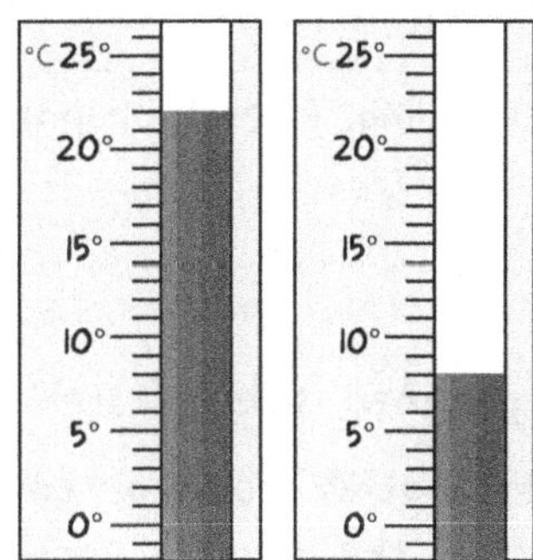

Answer ____________________

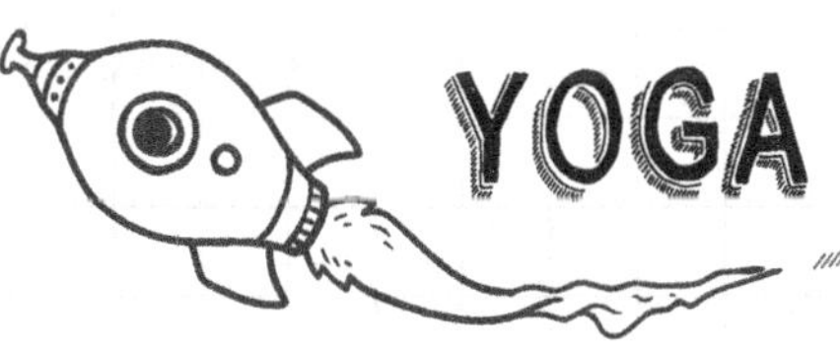

YOGA ☆

Please be aware of your environment and be safe at all times. If you cannot do an exercise, just try your best.

1 - Bend Down: 20 sec.

START

2 - Child Pose: 20 sec.

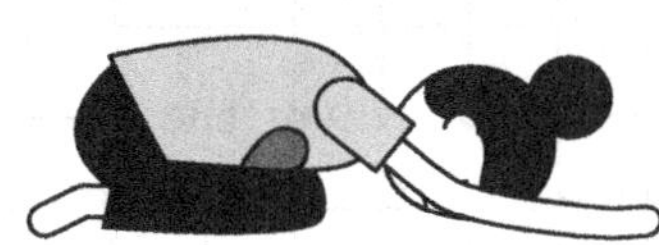

3 - Chair: 20 sec.

4 -Book Pose: 20 sec. Note: Keep your core tight. Legs shoud be across your eyes.

5 - Shavasana: as long as you can. Note: think of happy moments and relax your mind.

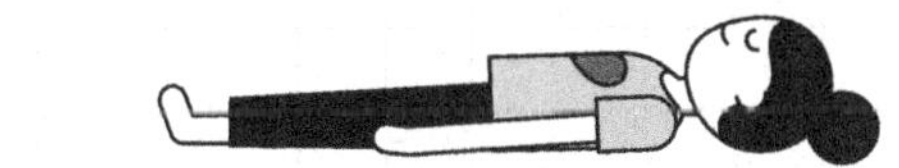

WEEK 5 DAY 6 EXPERIMENT

Identifying Materials Based on Properties

Last week, we saw that all objects made of matter have **properties**. That is, they have qualities or characteristics that we can observe. While it's important to be able to describe something's traits, it's also extremely valuable to work backwards and use a list of traits to figure out what object or item they're describing. Today, we'll reverse the process we used last week and use properties to identify objects.

Materials:

- 5 objects of different sizes, shapes, colors, etc. (nothing bigger than a basketball)
- 5 objects selected by somebody else (objects whose identities are secret to you) of different sizes, shapes, colors, etc. (nothing bigger than a basketball)
- A scale that can measure in grams or ounces (a kitchen scale is ideal)
- A ruler or flexible tape measure
- Notepaper
- A partner (like a sibling, friend, or parent)

Procedure:

1. Working with a partner, select **5** items together and set them aside.
2. While you wait in another room or cover your eyes, have your partner gather five **5** more objects from around the house without showing them to you.
3. While your partner looks for those **5** objects, use your ruler and notepaper to create a table just like the one from last week. It should look like this but have 10 different rows for various objects:

OBJECT	SHAPE	COLOR	WEIGHT	DIMENSIONS	MATERIALS
Baseball					
Nickel					
Saucer					
Etc.					

4. When your partner is done gathering their secret objects, give them the **five objects you chose together** and have them fill out the first five rows on the table you just made. It makes the activity more challenging if you're in another room for this part!
5. Once your partner has completed the descriptions of the objects you **have seen**, they should also use the ruler, scale, and other tools to complete the table for the objects you **haven't seen** as well. For these items, your partner should leave the **OBJECT** column empty so you don't know which items they're describing.
6. Once your partner has filled in the table, enter the room and look at the descriptions of the objects you chose together. Using your knowledge of properties, identify what each object is in the left-most column.

7. **Without looking at the mystery objects**, use their properties from the table to try to determine what they are. Start by looking at their color and what materials they're made out of, and be sure to consider their overall size as well. When you think you know what the object being described is, write your answer in the left column.
8. Once you've filled in all the blanks, have your partner reveal what the various secret items were, and see how well you did figuring them out. For items you identified correctly, think about which properties helped you find the answer fastest. For items you weren't able to identify, think about what other properties or information would've been useful to help you figure it out.

Follow-Up Questions:

1. How was identifying the materials based on their properties different from describing properties (like we did last week)?

___

___

___

2. Which objects (if any) that you hadn't seen before were you able to identify based on their properties? Which properties were most useful for helping you figure out what they were?

___

___

___

YOGA ☆

Please be aware of your environment and be safe at all times. If you cannot do an exercise, just try your best.

1 - Tree Pose: Stay as long as possible.
Note: do on one leg then on another.

2 - Down Dog: 20 sec.

3 - Shavasana: 15 min.
Note: this pose is very important and provides you with long term benefits. Try not to skip this. Close your eyes and imagine who you want to be and what your goals are! Always think happy thoughts.

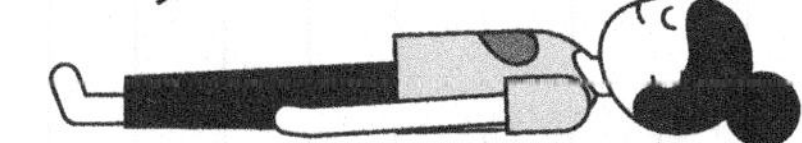

WEEK 5 DAY 7 MAZE

Task: The wires are messed up. Help music lovers by connecting the numbers of the headphones with the letters of the music players.

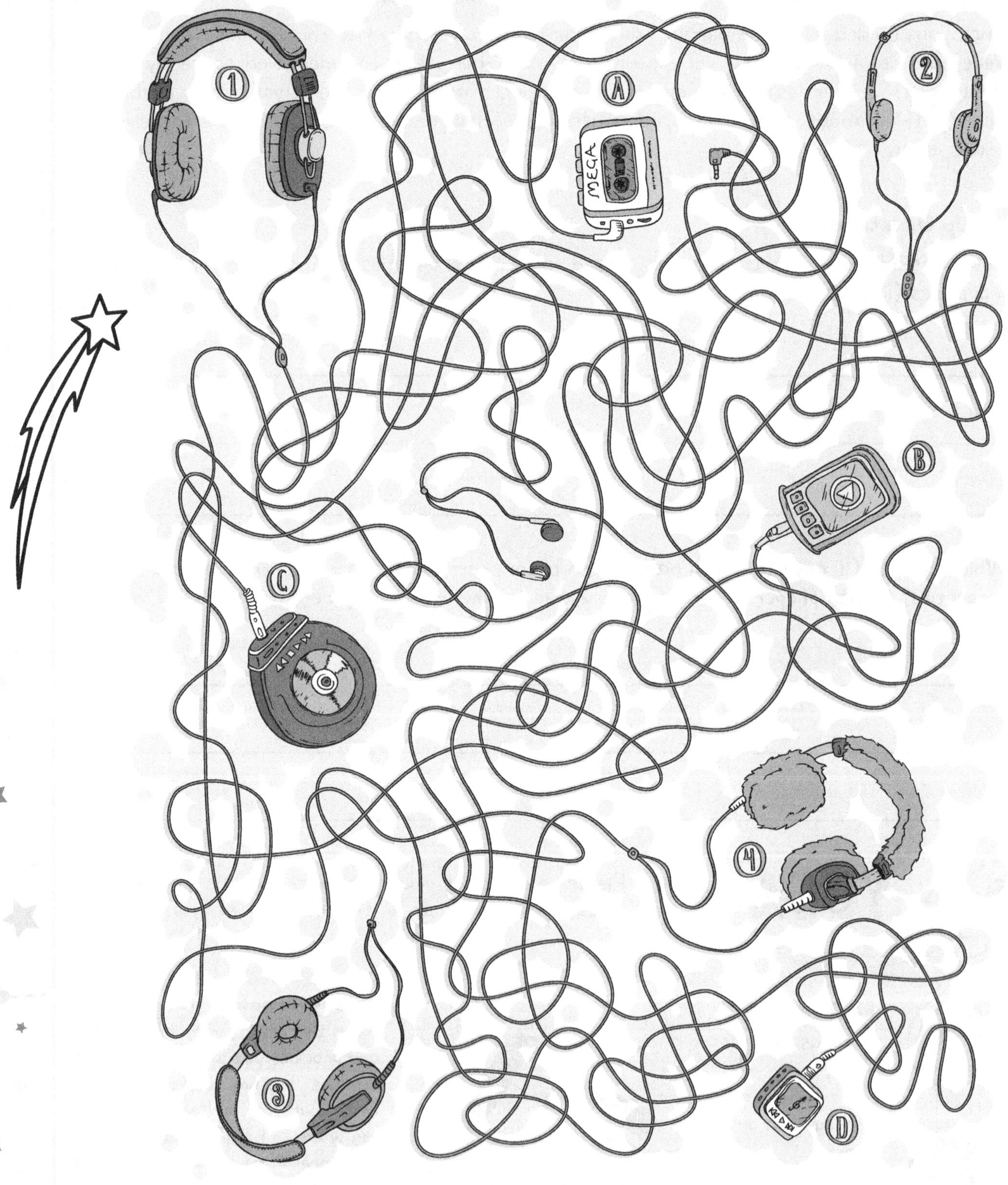

Answers: ___________________________

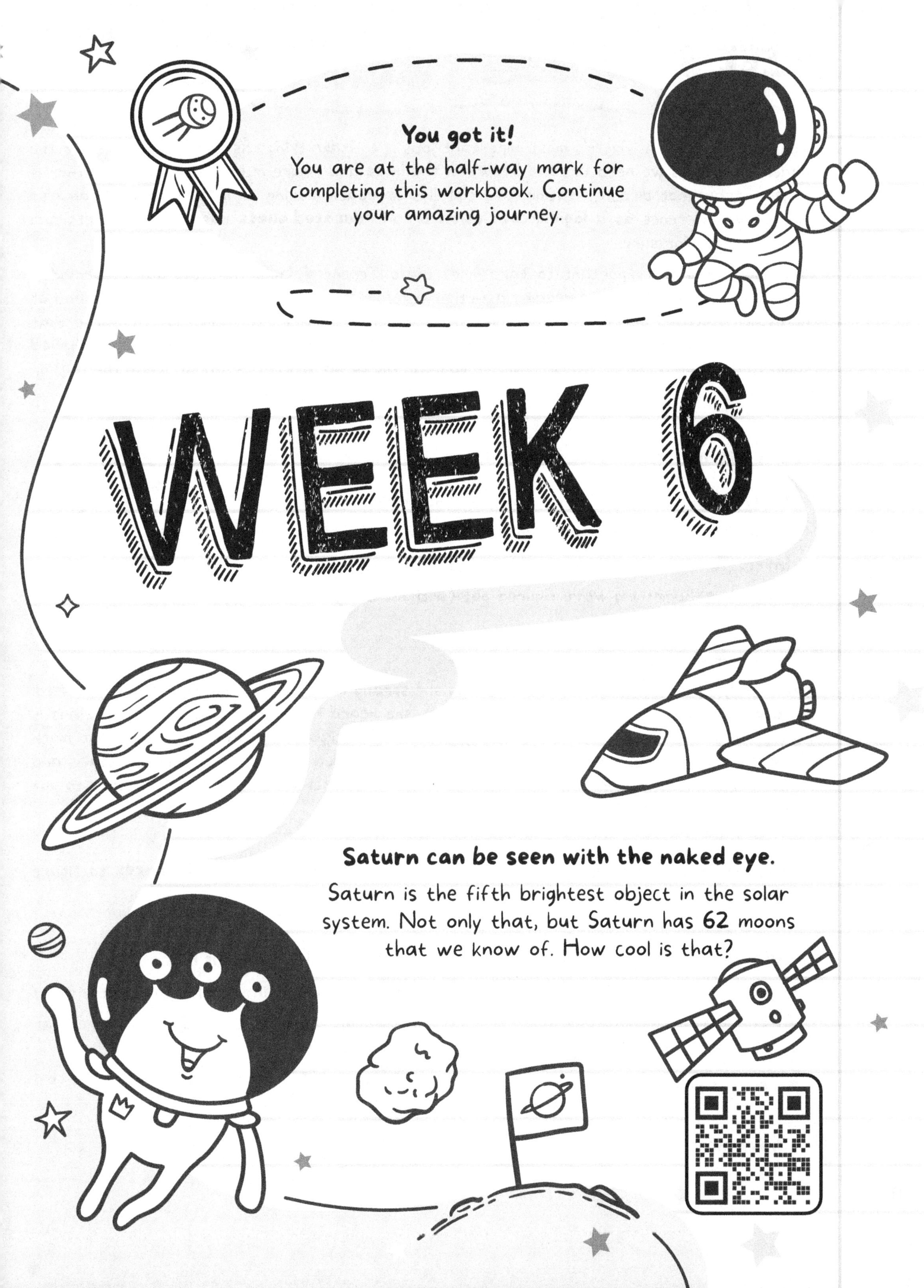
You got it!
You are at the half-way mark for completing this workbook. Continue your amazing journey.
WEEK 6
Saturn can be seen with the naked eye.
Saturn is the fifth brightest object in the solar system. Not only that, but Saturn has 62 moons that we know of. How cool is that?

WEEK 6 DAY 1  OVERVIEW OF ENGLISH CONCEPTS MAKING INFERENCES

Even though one of a writer's most important jobs is to make things as clear as possible for the reader, sometimes we need to **read between the lines** and figure out ideas that the author is suggesting, but not directly stating. We call this approach making an **inference**. You can also think of an inference as a **logical conclusion** or an **educated guess** based on the facts and ideas we know for sure.

When you read, it's important to take in all the different **details** that the author provides, regardless of whether you're reading a fiction text or a non-fiction text. Once you've read all the explicitly stated details, ask yourself, "Does it feel like there's anything going on here that the author is suggesting without saying outright?" If you feel like something is being **implied** (suggested), read again closely, and see if you can **make an inference** about what the author is saying.

Key Terms

Imply: To suggest something strongly without saying it directly

Implication: Something that is suggested by an author (but not directly said)

Infer: To make a conclusion based on evidence

Inference: Something we've figured out (without being told directly) based on evidence

For Example...

"When Sally saw the time on her alarm clock, she sprang out of bed and began getting dressed. She brushed her teeth as fast as she could, as she heard her mother call, "Honey, the bus is going to be here any minute!" She quickly grabbed her backpack, although she was in too much of a rush to double-check that she had everything she needed. She sprinted down the stairs and headed for the door before her mother handed over her lunchbox and warned, "Be sure to put on your hat and boots. It's going to be cold on the bus."

Even though the author didn't explain this situation fully, we can **make inferences** to figure out more about what's going on. **For example...**

Where is Sally going?

- Detail: She lives with her parents
- Detail: She is taking a bus
- Detail: She is bringing a backpack
- Detail: She is bringing a lunchbox

Inference: Sally is going to school!

What time of year is it?

- Detail: Sally is in school (we're pretty sure)
- Detail: Her mom tells her to wear her hat and boots
- Detail: Her mom says it's going to be cold on the bus

Inference: It must be winter!

From The Seventh Voyage of Sinbad

By E. Dixon

Being returned from my sixth voyage, I absolutely laid aside all thoughts of travelling any farther; for, besides that my years now required rest, I was resolved no more to expose myself to such risk as I had run; so that I thought of nothing but to pass the rest of my days in quiet. One day, as I was treating some of my friends, one of my servants came and told me that an officer of the caliph asked for me. I rose from the table, and went to him. "The caliph," said he, "has sent me to tell you that he must speak with you." I followed the officer to the palace, where, being presented to the caliph, I saluted him by prostrating myself at his feet. "Sinbad," said he to me, "I stand in need of you; you must do me the service to carry my answer and present to the King of Serendib. It is but just I should return his civility."

This command of the caliph to me was like a clap of thunder. "Commander of the Faithful," replied I, "I am ready to do whatever your majesty shall think fit to command me; but I beseech you most humbly to consider what I have undergone. I have also made a vow never to go out of Bagdad." Here I took occasion to give him a large and particular account of all my adventures, which he had the patience to hear out.

As soon as I had finished, "I confess," said he, "that the things you tell me are very extraordinary, yet you must for my sake undertake this voyage which I propose to you. You have nothing to do but to go to the Isle of Serendib, and deliver the commission which I give you. After that you are at liberty to return. But you must go; for you know it would be indecent, and not suitable to my dignity, to be indebted to the king of that island." Perceiving that the caliph insisted upon it, I submitted, and told him that I was willing to obey. He was very well pleased at it, and ordered me a thousand sequins for the expense of my journey.

I prepared for my departure in a few days, and as soon as the caliph's letter and present were delivered to me, I went to Balsora, where I embarked, and had a very happy voyage. I arrived at the Isle of Serendib, where I acquainted the king's ministers with my commission, and prayed them to get me speedy audience. They did so, and I was conducted to the palace in an honourable manner, where I saluted the king by prostration, according to custom. That prince knew me immediately, and testified very great joy to see me. "O Sinbad," said he, "you are welcome; I swear to you I have many times thought of you since you went hence; I bless the day upon which we see one another once more." I made my compliment to him, and after having thanked him for his kindness to me, I delivered the caliph's letter and present, which he received with all imaginable satisfaction.

1. Based on the first paragraph, what can we **infer** about the narrator's history or lifestyle?

____

____

2. What is the mission that the caliph gives Sinbad?

3. Based on context clues, what is a **"caliph"** (Paragraph 1)?

   A. A powerful and fearsome warrior
   B. A ruler or king-like figure
   C. A mythical beast
   D. A magician or wizard

4. Which of these is the best definition for "prostration" based on context clues (Paragraph 1 & Paragraph 4)?

   A. A bow down or show of respect
   B. Treasure
   C. Frustration
   D. Storytelling

5. How is Sinbad treated by the caliph and the king in the passage? What does this tell you about Sinbad's personality or reputation?

Making an Inference

Directions:

Read the sentences below. Then, on the lines underneath, answer the question by making an **inference** based on what you read, and circle the words or ideas in the sentence that provided you with hints.

1. Kelly stood outside the bathroom door, checking her watch.

"If we don't leave soon, we'll miss our reservation!" she called.

"Sorry," Sam replied. "I've never been to a place this fancy before. I just want to make sure I look good."

"Nobody's going to be focused on how you look if the food is as good as it's supposed to be!" Kelly assured him.

MAKE AN INFERENCE - WHERE ARE SAM & KELLY GOING?

(Be sure to circle the words in the story that were hints!)

____

____

2. Angie answered the doorbell and instantly held a finger over her lips.

"Come on in. He has no idea," she whispered to Chris.

"Do you have a place you want me to put this?" Chris whispered back, holding out a wrapped present with a big bow on it.

"Just put it in the table and head out back. Everybody is waiting outside. When he gets out of the shower and is dressed, I'll bring him out and we can all give him a good scare."

"Oh man!" Chris said in excitement. "This is going to be great! He has no idea."

MAKE AN INFERENCE - WHAT IS ABOUT TO HAPPEN? WHAT IS ANGIE UP TO?

(Be sure to circle the words in the story that were hints!)

____

____

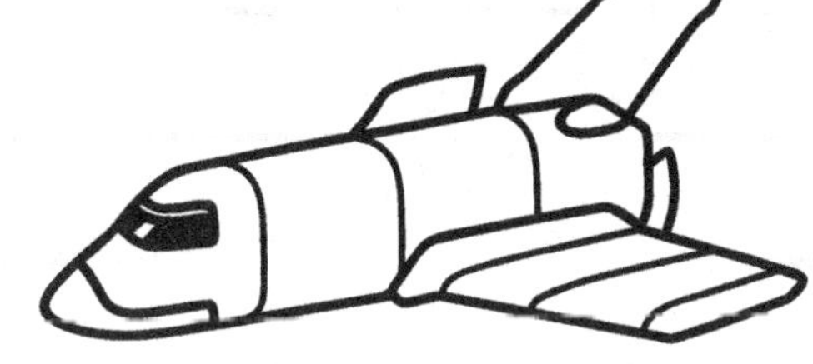

FITNESS

Please be aware of your environment and be safe at all times. If you cannot do an exercise, just try your best.

Repeat these exercises **3 ROUNDS**

1 - Bend forward: 10 times.
Note: try to touch your feet. Make sure to keep your back straight and if needed you can bend your knees.

2 - Abs: 10 times

3 - Plank: 15 sec.

4 - Run: 50m
Note: Run **25** meters to one side and **25** meters back to the starting position.

From The First Voyage of Sinbad

By E. Dixon

My father left me a considerable estate, the best part of which I spent in riotous living during my youth; but I perceived my error, and reflected that riches were perishable, and quickly consumed by such ill managers as myself. I further considered that by my irregular way of living I had wretchedly misspent my time which is the most valuable thing in the world. Struck with those reflections, I collected the remains of my furniture, and sold all my patrimony by public auction to the highest bidder. Then I entered into a contract with some merchants, who traded by sea. I took the advice of such as I thought most capable to give it me; and resolving to improve what money I had, I went to Balsora and embarked with several merchants on board a ship which we jointly fitted out.

We set sail, and steered our course towards the East Indies, through the Persian Gulf, which is formed by the coasts of Arabia Felix on the right, and by those of Persia on the left, and, according to common opinion, is seventy leagues across at the broadest part. The eastern sea, as well as that of the Indies, is very spacious: it is bounded on one side by the coasts of Abyssinia, and is 4,500 leagues in length to the isles of Vakvak. At first I was troubled with sea-sickness, but speedily recovered my health, and was not afterwards troubled with that disease.

In our voyage we touched at several islands, where we sold or exchanged our goods. One day, whilst under sail, we were becalmed near a little island, almost even with the surface of the water, which resembled a green meadow. The captain ordered his sails to be furled, and permitted such persons as had a mind to do so to land upon the island, amongst whom I was one.

WEEK 6 DAY 2 — READING PASSAGE: MAKING INFERENCES

1. Based on the passage, what was the narrator, Sinbad, like when he was **young**?

____

____

2. Based on his decision to give up everything and become a sailor, what can we **infer** about Sinbad?

____

____

____

____

3. What can we **infer** based on Sinbad's sea-sickness?

   A. He is weak
   B. He is going to have a tough journey
   C. He is not an experienced traveler
   D. He is cursed

4. What doe Sinbad decide to do at the end of the passage?

   A. Give up being a sailor
   B. Become a pirate
   C. Take over as the captain of the ship
   D. Get off the boat to explore an island

5. What details or ideas from the text support the **inference** that something unexpected or bad will happen on the island Sinbad is visiting?

____

____

____

____

Assessing an Inference

Directions:

Read each group of sentences, and then take a look at the inference another student made after reading. Decide whether you **agree** or **disagree** with the inference, based on the text, and explain why.

1. Unicorns are mythical creatures that, in most depictions, look like a horse with a single horn in the middle of its forehead. Unicorns symbolize magic, innocence, beauty, and mystery in many ancient stories and works of art. During medieval times, there were several attempts to catch and tame unicorns, but of course, none of those hunts were ever successful. In today's world, the term "unicorn" is often used to represent something unattainable or impossibly perfect.

HERE'S AN INFERENCE: After reading this, one student **inferred** that unicorns used to exist in the past, but they do not anymore.

Do you agree? ___________________________

What ideas from the text make you agree or disagree? ___________________________

____

____

____

2. Red tide occurs when certain algae that live in coastal water reproduce so dramatically that they actually discolor the water. Although red tides are possible in various different parts of the world, they are most associated with Florida. When sea water is filled with these red algae, it actually reduces the amount of oxygen in the water, which can choke fish and other sea life to death. Some of the algae associated with red tide even produce mild toxins that aren't poisonous in small amounts but can be dangerous when many algae are concentrated in one place.

HERE'S AN INFERENCE: After reading this, one student **inferred** it would **not** be safe to swim at a beach where red tide was occurring.

Do you agree? ________________________

What ideas from the text make you agree or disagree? ______________________

____

____

____

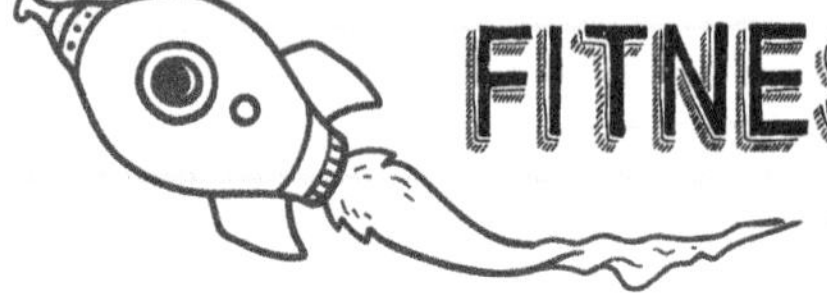

FITNESS

Please be aware of your environment and be safe at all times. If you cannot do an exercise, just try your best.

Repeat these exercises **3 ROUNDS**

1 - Squats: 15 times. Note: imagine you are trying to sit on a chair.

2 - Side Bending: 10 times to each side. Note: try to touch your feet.

3 - Tree Pose: Stay as long as possible. Note: do the same with the other leg.

MATH

Rewriting fractions as decimals

1. Convert the fraction $\frac{64}{100}$ into a decimal.

   A. 0.604
   B. 0.064
   C. 6.40
   D. 0.64

2. Which fraction is equivalent to 0.307?

   A. $3\frac{7}{1,000}$
   B. $37\frac{1}{1,000}$
   C. $\frac{307}{1,000}$
   D. $\frac{37}{1,000}$

3. How can $6\frac{5}{10}$ be written as a decimal?

   A. 6.5
   B. 0.65
   C. 6.05
   D. 60.5

4. Convert the fraction $\frac{75}{1,000}$ into a decimal.

   A. 0.075
   B. 0.705
   C. 0.750
   D. 7.005

5. What is $5\frac{6}{100}$ rewritten as a decimal?

   A. 5.60
   B. 5.06
   C. 0.56
   D. 0.506

6. Which decimal is equivalent to $\frac{3}{6}$?

   A. 3.6
   B. 0.36
   C. 0.5
   D. 3.06

7. Write a decimal that is equivalent to $\frac{108}{1,000}$.

   Answer ______________________

8. $\frac{38}{100}$ can be written in decimal form as:

   Answer ______________________

9. Write a decimal that is equivalent to $3\frac{42}{1,000}$.

   Answer ______________________

10. Convert the fraction $2\frac{1}{2}$ into a decimal.

   Answer ______________________

Improper Fractions vs. Mixed Fractions

1. The fraction $7\frac{4}{8}$ can be rewritten as:

   A. $\frac{74}{8}$
   B. $\frac{56}{5}$
   C. $\frac{60}{8}$
   D. $\frac{68}{8}$

WEEK 6 DAY 3  MATH

2. What is another way to write $\frac{51}{7}$?

   A. $5\frac{1}{7}$

   B. $7\frac{2}{7}$

   C. $6\frac{4}{7}$

   D. $7\frac{5}{7}$

3. Which number sentence is true?

   A. $\frac{28}{9} = 3\frac{1}{3}$

   B. $7\frac{3}{5} < \frac{50}{10}$

   C. $5\frac{7}{8} > \frac{20}{4}$

   D. $\frac{16}{5} = 3\frac{1}{2}$

4. What fraction completes the number sentence ___ $= 3\frac{2}{16}$ to make it true?

   A. $\frac{25}{8}$

   B. $\frac{51}{16}$

   C. $\frac{26}{8}$

   D. $\frac{14}{4}$

5. Which number sentence is true?

   A. $3\frac{7}{12} = \frac{44}{12}$

   B. $5\frac{4}{7} = \frac{36}{7}$

   C. $2\frac{7}{15} = \frac{42}{15}$

   D. $6\frac{7}{9} = \frac{61}{9}$

6. Compare the fractions $4\frac{3}{8}$ ___ $\frac{16}{4}$, using $<$, $>$ or $=$ symbols.

7. Rewrite $\frac{65}{12}$ as a mixed fraction.

   Answer ______________________

8. Rewrite $12\frac{25}{8}$ as an improper fraction.

   Answer ______________________

9. Compare the fractions $5\frac{17}{25}$ ___ $\frac{32}{5}$, using $<$, $>$ or $=$ symbols.

10. Rewrite $8\frac{7}{8}$ as an improper fraction.

    Answer ______________________

FITNESS ☆

Please be aware of your environment and be safe at all times. If you cannot do an exercise, just try your best.

Today you get to decide which exercises you would like to do! Think of the previous exercises and select which fitness activity you would like to do.

WEEK 6 DAY 4

MATH

Placing fractions on a number line

1. Where is the point located on the number line?

A. $\frac{1}{3}$

B. $1\frac{1}{3}$

C. $\frac{5}{3}$

D. $1\frac{2}{3}$

2. Find the missing fraction on the number line.

A. $\frac{1}{6}$

B. $\frac{3}{6}$

C. $\frac{4}{6}$

D. $\frac{5}{6}$

3. Find the value of k.

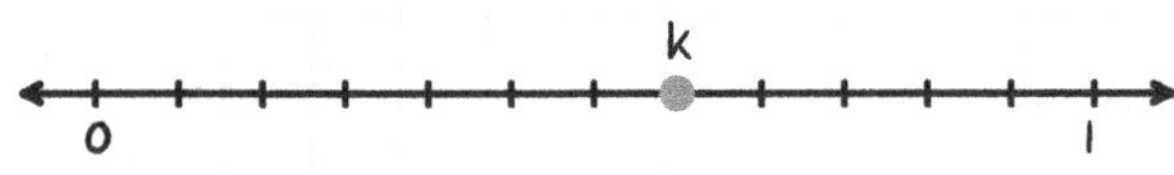

A. $\frac{1}{2}$

B. $\frac{5}{7}$

C. $\frac{5}{12}$

D. $\frac{7}{12}$

4. Which fraction represents one equal part of this number line?

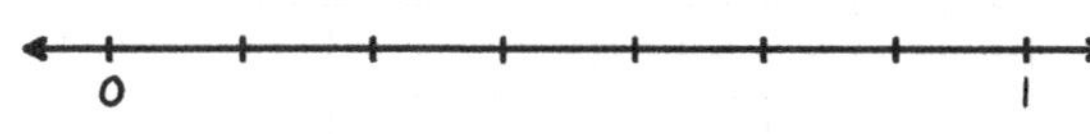

A. $\frac{1}{4}$

B. $\frac{1}{5}$

C. $\frac{1}{6}$

D. $\frac{1}{7}$

5. Find the missing number on the number line.

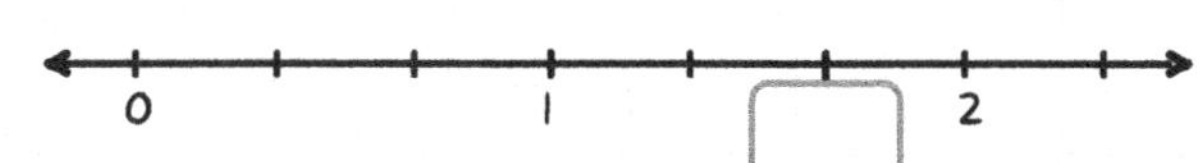

A. $\frac{2}{3}$

B. $1\frac{1}{3}$

C. $1\frac{2}{3}$

D. 2

6. What number does the letter F on the number line represent?

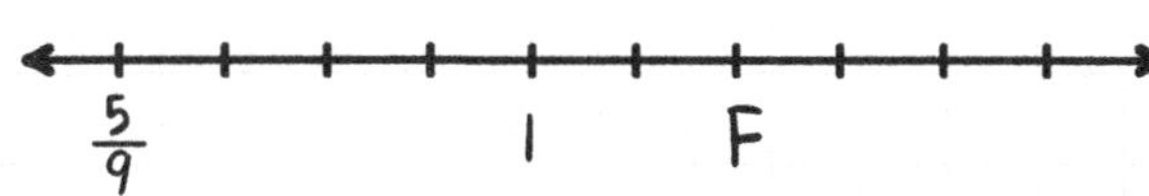

A. $1\frac{1}{9}$

B. $1\frac{2}{9}$

C. $1\frac{3}{9}$

D. $1\frac{4}{9}$

7. Plot the missing number on the number line.

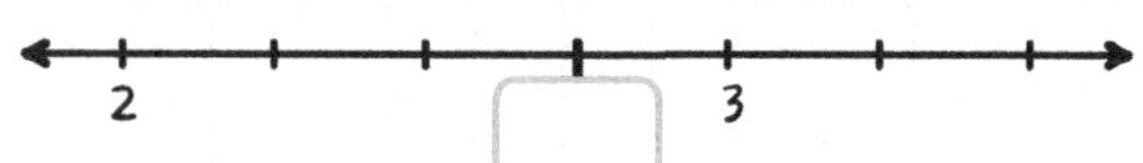

8. Draw the dot at $\frac{5}{12}$ on the number line.

9. Graph $1\frac{3}{5}$ as point K on the number line.

10. What numbers do the letters K, L, M on the number line represent?

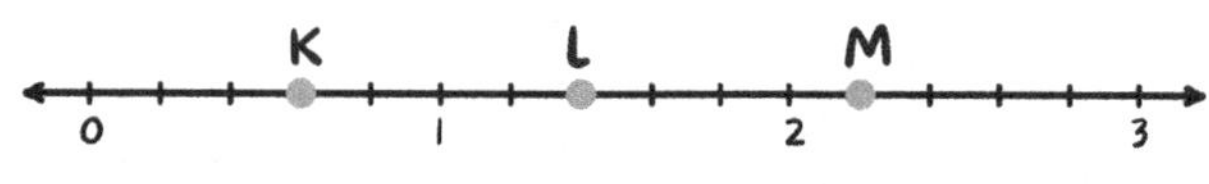

Answer ______________________

Various Real World Word Problems

1. A company supplies a school with 565 pens. The pens are divided evenly among 8 groups. The rest of the pens are given to the library. How many pens were donated to each group and to the library?

   Answer ______________________

   ____

2. Gerard owns 39 sets of basketball cards. Each set has exactly 420 cards. What is the total number of basketball cards Gerard owns?

   A. 15,400
   B. 15,960
   C. 16,380
   D. 16,540

Please be aware of your environment and be safe at all times. If you cannot do an exercise, just try your best.

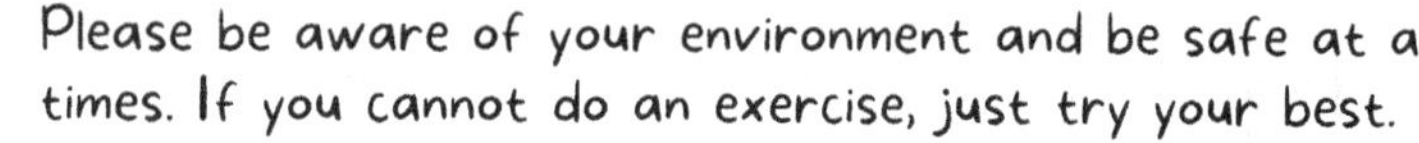

Repeat these exercises **3 ROUNDS**

1 - High Plank: 15 sec.

2 - Abs: 10 times

3 - Side Bending: 10 times to each side. Note: try to touch your feet.

  MATH

Various Real World Word Problems

1. The city park is $5\frac{4}{5}$ miles from Forest Elementary School. The city library is $3\frac{3}{5}$ miles from the same school. How much farther from the school is the park than the library?

   Answer ____________________

2. Jane paid $4 and 23¢ for a sandwich. She also paid $1 and 90¢ each for two pieces of fruit. What is the total amount Jane paid for the sandwich and fruits?

   Answer ____________________

3. Betsy ate $\frac{1}{4}$ of a pepperoni pizza, and Victor ate $\frac{5}{12}$ of the same pizza. What fraction of the pizza did Betsy and Victor eat?

   A. $\frac{3}{4}$
   B. $\frac{8}{12}$
   C. $\frac{1}{3}$
   D. $\frac{6}{12}$

There are 8 doctors working in a clinic. Each doctor has 2 nurses assisting them. There are three receptionists: Craig, Linda and Monique. Solve questions 4 - 8.

4. How many people are working in the clinic?

   Answer ____________________

5. On Tuesday, 14 patients made appointments with each doctor. However, 16 of the patients did not show up. How many patients visited the clinic on Tuesday?

   Answer ____________________

6. On Monday, Linda answered 56 phone calls and Monique answered 17 more calls than Linda did. How many calls were answered in total?

   Answer ____________________

7. On Thursday, a doctor called in sick. Two of the receptionists, Craig and Linda had to call 45 patients to reschedule their appointments. If Craig called two times more patients than Linda, how many calls did Linda make?

   Answer ____________________

8. Among the calls they made, 21 of the patients decided to cancel their appointments, and the rest decided to postpone their appointments. How many appointments were postponed?

   Answer ____________________

9. In 2017, the population of a town was 56,128. In 2018, the population increased by 2,349. In 2018, the population is...

   A. 58,437
   B. 58,477
   C. 58,597
   D. 58,627

Right, Acute, Obtuse Angles

Use the drawing below to answer questions 1 through 3.

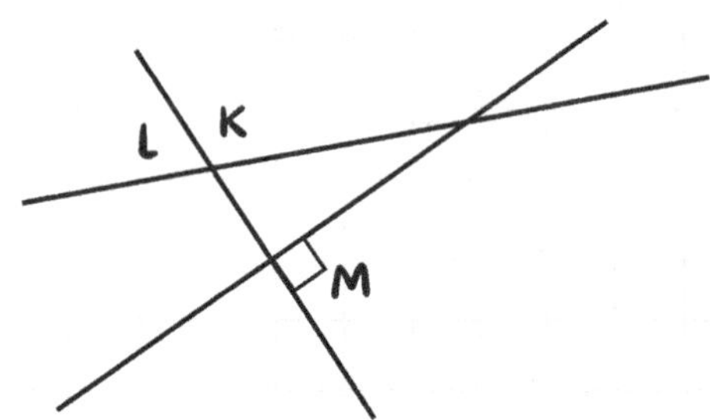

1. Which angle is an acute angle? ______

2. Which angle is an obtuse angle? ______

3. Which angle is a right angle? ______

4. For the figure below, count the number of angles for each type.

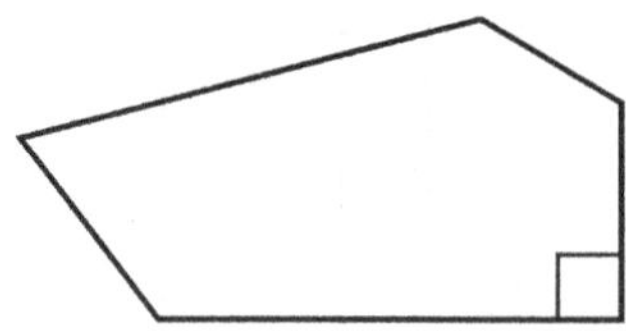

Number of acute angles ______

Number of obtuse angles ______

Number of right angles ______

5. Look at the angle marked on this shape:

What type of angle is it?

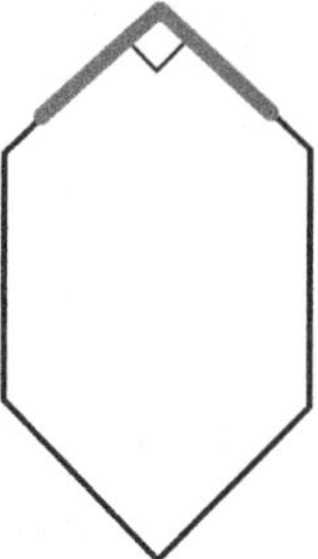

A. Acute
B. Obtuse
C. Right
D. None of the above

Use the shapes below to answer questions 6 through 8.

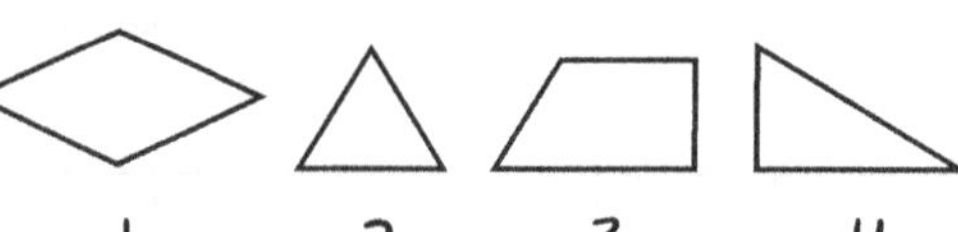

6. Which shapes have at least one acute angle?

Answer ____________________

7. Which shapes have at least one obtuse angle?

Answer ____________________

8. Which shapes have at least one right angle?

Answer ____________________

Please be aware of your environment and be safe at all times. If you cannot do an exercise, just try your best.

1 - Tree Pose: Stay as long as possible.
Note: do on one leg then on another.

2 - Down Dog: 20 sec.

3 - Shavasana: 15 min.
Note: this pose is very important and provides you with long term benefits. Try not to skip this. Close your eyes and imagine who you want to be and what your goals are! Always think happy thoughts.

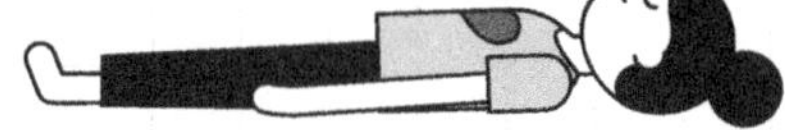

WEEK 6 DAY 6 EXPERIMENT

Physical vs. Chemical Change

We've talked a lot about properties of matter, but it would be a mistake to think that those properties never change. As objects get older and interact with other objects in their environment, they can change over time. In science, we classify the ways matter changes as either **physical** or **chemical** changes.

Physical changes affect how something looks. For example, if you cut the corner off a piece of paper, that would be a physical change because the paper looks different, but is still a piece of paper (just a slightly smaller piece of paper). On the other hand, if you burned that piece of paper, that would be a **chemical** change because you're turning the paper into light, heat, and a pile of ash. Since the product of that process is **not** paper, that's a chemical change - a change to the actual structure or nature of an object! Usually, you can tell if a chemical change is happening if there is a color change, an odor created, or light, bubbles, or sound being emitted.

Materials:

- Two eggs
- A small cooking pot
- A stovetop or range (be sure to ask your parents for help)
- A teacup or small bowl
- A fork
- A small skillet
- A sink with running water
- Notepaper

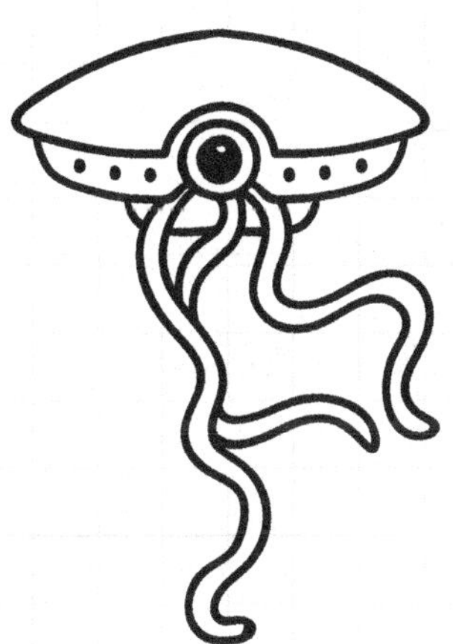

Procedure:

1. Break one of the two eggs into the teacup or small bowl and, on your notepaper, write a short description of what the egg looks like.
2. Using your fork, pierce the yolk of the egg in the bowl and stir or whip the egg rapidly for about thirty seconds. On your notepaper, write a short description of how the egg has changed.
3. Ask yourself: "Was what I just did to that egg a **physical** or **chemical** change?" Did I alter how the egg was made or what it was made up of, or did I just change how it looks? Write your thoughts in your notes.
4. Set that egg aside for a few minutes (you can cover the bowl and put it in the refrigerator for safety).
5. Carefully place the remaining whole egg in the small cookpot and fill the pot with water until it covers the egg by at least an inch.
6. With help from a parent, put the pot on the stove uncovered and set the burner to high.
7. When the water boils, cover the pan, take it off the heat, and allow it to sit for 10 minutes.
8. Carefully remove the egg from the water and peel it once it is cool enough (a quick dip in some ice water can be helpful to loosen the shell).

EXPERIMENT

9. Using your notepaper, write a few notes about what the egg looks like now and ask yourself: "Was what I just did to that egg a **physical** or **chemical** change?" If the egg is cooled, you can also cut it to observe what happened inside.
10. Take the raw scrambled egg out of the fridge and think about how it is different from your hard-boiled egg. See if you notice any **smells or color changes** that show a chemical change has taken place with either one.
11. Once you've written your observations down in your notes, you can also cook and eat the scrambled egg to avoid waste.

Follow-Up Questions:

1. What is the biggest indicator or hint that the hard-boiled egg has been through a chemical change, while the raw scrambled egg has not?

____

____

____

2. Based on what you saw with the egg, how is **cooking** related to the idea of a **chemical change**?

____

____

____

YOGA

Please be aware of your environment and be safe at all times. If you cannot do an exercise, just try your best.

1 - Bend Down: 20 sec.

START

2 - Child Pose: 20 sec.

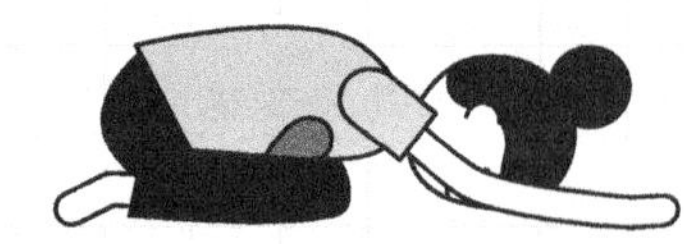

3 - Chair: 20 sec.

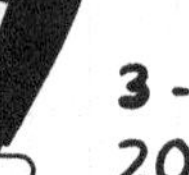

4 - Book Pose: 20 sec. Note: Keep your core tight. Legs shoud be across your eyes.

5 - Shavasana: as long as you can. Note: think of happy moments and relax your mind.

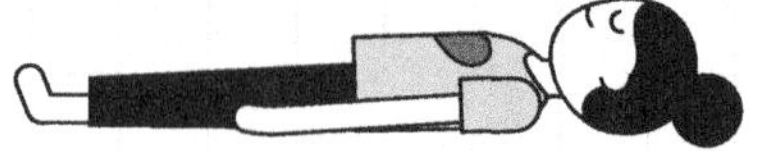

  MAZE

Task: Anchor chains got tangled after the storm. Help the boats find their anchors.

1 2 3 4

B A C D E F

Answers: ___________________________

That was easy!
Your mission on Saturn was perfectly accomplished. Time to go to Uranus.

WEEK 7

Uranus has the coldest temperatures of any planet.

It's freezing on planet Uranus!
Just to give you an idea, the minimum atmospheric temperature is -224° C.

WEEK 7 DAY 1

OVERVIEW OF ENGLISH CONCEPTS
IDENTIFYING MAIN IDEAS IN NONFICTION TEXTS

Nonfiction texts explore key ideas from real life, such as science, history, and reports of events that are unfolding around the world. Nonfiction texts are designed to be very **focused** on the specific topic or idea they're describing or explaining. One of the most important skills as a reader of nonfiction texts is the ability to determine the author's point, perspective, or main idea as quickly as possible.

As you start to read more advanced texts, getting down to the heart of the issue gets a little trickier because of the addition of complex sentences and high-level vocabulary. If you use these key strategies, though, you'll be finding main ideas in no time!

Key Strategies:

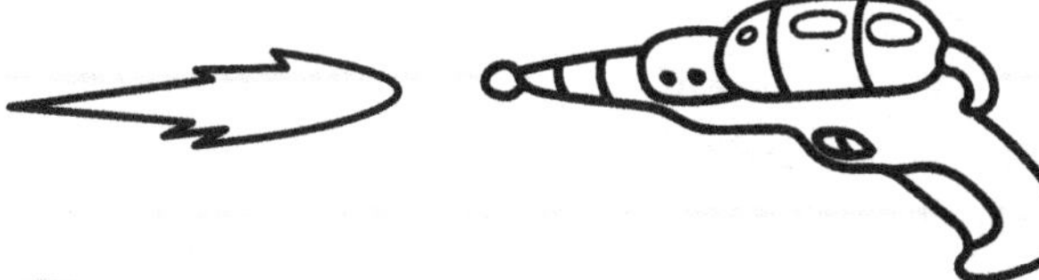

- Look at the **title** or **headings** (if there are any)
  - If an author is organized, they should provide the reader with a title that lets them know **exactly** what they're getting into
  - If you're reading a highly structured text (like a school textbook), there will probably be **section headings** that should tell you what each part of the text is talking about
- Search for **repeated words and ideas**
  - Authors use repetition to emphasize points
  - If an idea or word is repeated several times throughout the text, it's probably key to understanding what's going on!
- Pay close attention to the **first and last** sentences of each paragraph and the first and last **paragraphs** of the text or section of text
  - The beginning and the end are the places where the author should be **previewing** and **reviewing** ideas. The clearest articulation of their point should be in one of those spots
- Once you think you've arrived at the main idea, **read back through the text again** to confirm your thinking.
  - If what you thought was the main idea doesn't seem to come up a lot during your second reading, you might want to adjust your thinking!

As always, the real secret is to **read closely, carefully, and multiple times** to ensure you're understanding both the text as a whole and the individual smaller points the author makes throughout the text.

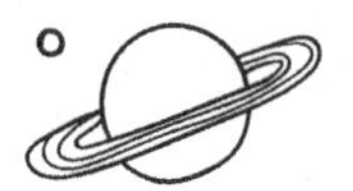

From "Rembrandt and His Works"

By John Burnet

The mother of Rembrandt was Neeltje Willems Van Zuitbroek, whose portrait he has etched. As he was an only child, his parents were anxious to give him a good education, and therefore sent him to the Latin school at Leyden, in order to bring him up to the profession of the law; but, like our own inimitable Shakespeare, he picked up "small Latin and less Greek." Having shown an early inclination for painting, they placed him under the tuition of Jacob Van Zwaanenburg, a painter unmentioned by any biographer; he afterwards entered the studio of Peter Lastman, and finally received instruction from Jacob Pinas. The two last had visited Rome, but, notwithstanding, could have given little instruction to Rembrandt, as their works show no proof of their having studied the Italian school to much purpose.

After receiving a knowledge of a few rules, such as they could communicate, he returned home, and commenced painting from nature, when he laid the foundation of a style in art unapproached either before his time or since. In 1627 he is said, by Houbraken, to have visited the Hague, when, by the price he received for one of his pictures, he discovered his value as an artist. The neighborhood of the Rhine was now given up for the city of Amsterdam, where he set up his easel in the year 1628, under the patronage of the Burgomaster Six, and other wealthy admirers of the fine arts.

Rembrandt's first works, like all the early works of eminent artists, were carefully finished; the work that raised him to the greatest notice, in the first instance, is Professor Tulpius giving an Anatomical Lecture on a dead Body, and is dated 1632.

1. How could the author have made the topic of the passage **more clear** in Paragraph 1?

2. What does the author think about Rembrandt's teachers? Does he believe they were important to Rembrandt becoming great, or were they just lucky to have him as a student? What from the text makes you say that?

3. Who is the main person being described in the **first** paragraph?

A. Rembrandt's Mother
B. Rembrandt's teacher
C. Rembrandt
D. Shakespeare

4. Which of these best describes the main idea of the second paragraph?

A. Between 1627 and 1628, Rembrandt traveled to several different places and began to build his reputation as a great artist.
B. Between 1627 and 1628, Rembrandt created his most important paintings.
C. Between 1627 and 1628, Rembrandt learned how to be a great artist from a series of teachers.
D. Between 1627 and 1628, Rembrandt regretted his choice to become an artist.

5. In your own words, what were the main ideas of this passage?

____

____

____

____

____

____

Identifying the Main Idea

Directions:

Each set of sentences below is related to one main idea. Read each set of sentences carefully. Then, on the line below, write the main idea that you think all four sentences are connected to.

1. (A) Sophie won the school spelling bee last year.
   (B) Sophie is an excellent field hockey player.
   (C) Sophie is respectful to her teachers.
   (D) Sophie always does her homework.

MAIN IDEA: ____

____

2. (A) In football, almost every play requires that players tackle each other to the ground.
   (B) Football players frequently bash heads together, both by accident and on purpose.
   (C) Many football players deal with long-term health problems related to football after their playing careers are over.
   (D) The average professional football career is only 3 or 4 years long, mostly because of injuries.

MAIN IDEA: ____

____

3. (A) The ability to type fast makes it much easier to take notes as someone is talking.
   (B) Proper typing techniques allow people to use computers more efficiently and effectively.
   (C) Typing skills are an expectation for most office jobs.
   (D) The ability to type well eliminates confusion over bad handwriting and creates clearer, better organized documents.

MAIN IDEA: ____

____

FITNESS

Please be aware of your environment and be safe at all times. If you cannot do an exercise, just try your best.

Repeat these exercises **3 ROUNDS**

1 - Bend forward: 10 times.
Note: try to touch your feet. Make sure to keep your back straight and if needed you can bend your knees.

2 - Abs: 10 times

3 - Plank: 15 sec.

4 - Run: 50m
Note: Run 25 meters to one side and 25 meters back to the starting position.

From "Ancient Egypt"

By Arthur Gilman

In shape Egypt is like a lily with a crooked stem. A broad blossom terminates it at its upper end; a button of a bud projects from the stalk a little below the blossom, on the left-hand side. The broad blossom is the Delta, extending from Aboosir to Tineh, a direct distance of a hundred and eighty miles, which the projection of the coast - the graceful swell of the petals - enlarges to two hundred and thirty. The bud is the Fayoum, a natural depression in the hills that shut in the Nile valley on the west, which has been rendered cultivable for many thousands of years by the introduction into it of the Nile water, through a canal known as the "Bahr Yousouf". The long stalk of the lily is the Nile valley itself, which is a ravine scooped in the rocky soil for seven hundred miles from the First Cataract to the apex of the Delta, sometimes not more than a mile broad, never more than eight or ten miles. No other country in the world is so strangely shaped, so long compared to its width, so straggling, so hard to govern from a single centre.

At the first glance, the country seems to divide itself into two strongly contrasted regions; and this was the original impression which it made upon its inhabitants. The natives from a very early time designated their land as "the two lands", and represented it by a hieroglyph in which the form used to express "land" was doubled. The kings were called "chiefs of the Two Lands", and wore two crowns, as being kings of two countries. The Hebrews caught up the idea, and though they sometimes called Egypt "Mazor" in the singular number, preferred commonly to designate it by the dual form "Mizraim", which means "the two Mazors". These "two Mazors," "two Egypts," or "two lands," were, of course, the blossom and the stalk, the broad tract upon the Mediterranean known as "Lower Egypt," or "the Delta," and the long narrow valley that lies, like a green snake, to the south, which bears the name of "Upper Egypt," or "the Said." Nothing is more striking than the contrast between these two regions.

1. How were the kings of ancient Egypt kings of two countries?

____

____

2. According to the author, why was Egypt hard to rule or govern from any one main city?

____

____

3. What is the main idea or goal of the first paragraph?

A. Egypt's history
B. Egypt's culture
C. Egypt's government
D. Egypt's geography

4. What is the main idea or goal of the second paragraph?

A. Egypt's history
B. Egypt's culture
C. Egypt's government
D. Egypt's geography

5. Based on the final sentence of the passage, what kind of content or information would you expect to come next in Ancient Egypt?

____

____

____

____

____

____

Identifying the Main Idea
Part 2

Directions:

Each set of sentences below is related to one main idea. Read each set of sentences carefully. Then, on the line below, write the main idea that you think all four sentences are connected to.

1. (A) Halloween is the only holiday where you get to dress up in scary costumes.
   (B) On Halloween, everybody has to give you free candy, not just your family.
   (C) Halloween allows kids to blow off some steam and act crazy for one night.
   (D) On other holidays, you are supposed to spend time with your family, but Halloween is all about kids having fun.

MAIN IDEA: ____

____

2. (A) Electric cars reduce pollution because they emit far less exhaust than traditional gas engines.
   (B) Many electric vehicle charging stations are popping up in parking lots around the country.
   (C) Researchers estimate that by the year 2040, an electric car will be just as affordable as a traditional car.
   (D) Electric cars actually have much lower long-term costs than normal cars.

MAIN IDEA: ____

____

3. (A) Origami Club is the most popular club at our school.
   (B) People have been folding paper into Origami since the 1600s.
   (C) Although the practice began in Japan, Origami spread worldwide beginning in the 1850s.
   (D) Many people find Origami relaxing to do and love the miniature paper sculptures they create.

MAIN IDEA: ____

____

FITNESS

Please be aware of your environment and be safe at all times. If you cannot do an exercise, just try your best.

Repeat these exercises **3 ROUNDS**

1 - Squats: 15 times. Note: imagine you are trying to sit on a chair.

2 - Side Bending: 10 times to each side. Note: try to touch your feet.

3 - Tree Pose: Stay as long as possible. Note: do the same with the other leg.

4 - High Plank: 15 sec.

Fraction word problems

1. Fred had 60 toys he didn't play with. He donated $\frac{4}{6}$ of the toys to the fundraiser fair. How many toys did Fred keep?

   Answer ______________________

2. Ammy had $3\frac{2}{5}$ cups of cocoa powder. If she used $1\frac{3}{5}$ cups of the cocoa powder to bake brownies, how much cocoa powder did she have left?

   A. $2\frac{1}{5}$
   B. $1\frac{4}{5}$
   C. $1\frac{1}{5}$
   D. $\frac{4}{5}$

3. A group of eight friends each received four-twelfths of a pound of biscuits. How much biscuits did all the friends receive in total?

   A. $1\frac{9}{12}$ lb
   B. $3\frac{1}{12}$ lb
   C. $2\frac{3}{12}$ lb
   D. $2\frac{8}{12}$ lb

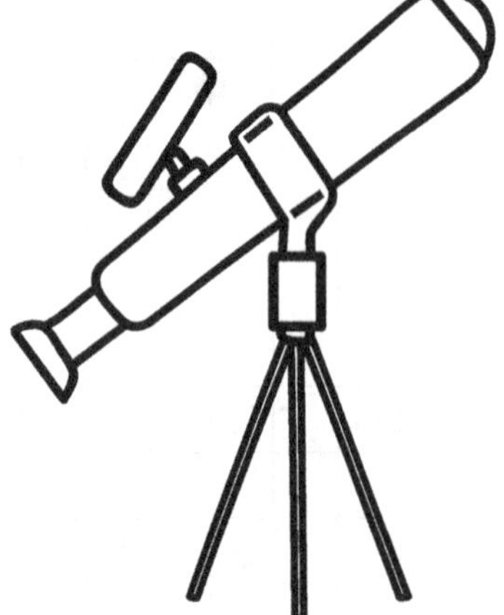

4. Ellie gave $\frac{3}{8}$ of her bracelets to her younger sister. She also gave $\frac{1}{2}$ of her bracelets to her friend Julie. Betsy got the rest of the bracelets. What fraction of the bracelets did Betsy get?

   A. $\frac{1}{8}$
   B. $\frac{2}{8}$
   C. $\frac{3}{8}$
   D. $\frac{4}{8}$

5. On Tuesday, it snowed fifteen centimeters. On Thursday, it snowed one-third of that amount. How much did it snow on Thursday?

   Answer ______________________

6. Aiden has read $\frac{3}{4}$ of a new magazine. There are 92 pages altogether. Bettany has read $\frac{4}{6}$ of another magazine that had a total of 96 pages.

   A. How many pages has Aiden read?
   B. How many pages has Bettany read?
   C. How many more pages did Aiden read than Bettany?

7. Chloe was packing up some of her toys into a box. A box can hold 12 pounds, but she only filled it up one-quarter full. How much did the box weigh?

   Answer ______________________

  MATH

8. Liza's kitten weighed $\frac{3}{5}$ kilograms. In two weeks it had gained another $\frac{4}{5}$ of a kilogram. What is the weight of the kitten currently?

   Answer ____________________

9. Declan stacked fourteen boxes on top of one another. If each box was three-fifths of a yard tall, how tall was the pile?

   A. $7\frac{3}{5}$
   B. $7\frac{4}{5}$
   C. $8\frac{2}{5}$
   D. $8\frac{3}{5}$

10. Benjamin bought wood at the hardware store. He used $\frac{3}{6}$ of the wood on a small chair. He used $\frac{2}{8}$ of the wood to make a shelf. What fraction of the wood was left?

   A. $\frac{1}{2}$
   B. $\frac{1}{4}$
   C. $\frac{1}{6}$
   D. $\frac{1}{8}$

11. A chef bought $5\frac{4}{7}$ pounds of onions. If he later bought another $4\frac{6}{7}$ pounds of onions, what is the total weight of the onions he bought?

   A. $9\frac{3}{7}$
   B. $9\frac{6}{7}$
   C. $10\frac{1}{7}$
   D. $10\frac{3}{7}$

FITNESS

☆ Please be aware of your environment and be safe at all times. If you cannot do an exercise, just try your best.

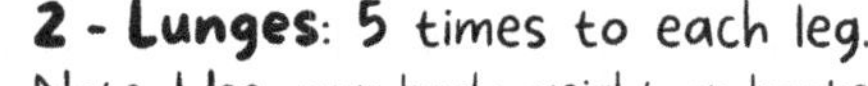

Repeat these exercises
3 ROUNDS

1 - Bend forward: 10 times.
Note: try to touch your feet. Make sure to keep your back straight and if needed you can bend your knees.

2 - Lunges: 5 times to each leg.
Note: Use your body weight or books as weight to do leg lunges.

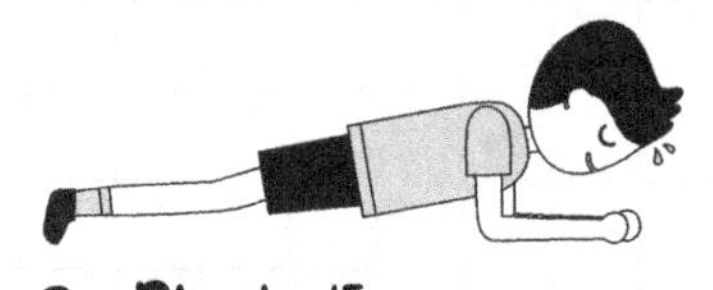

3 - Plank: 15 sec.

Fraction word problems

1. Todd spent $\frac{3}{12}$ of an hour learning a rhyme. Flo spent $\frac{2}{6}$ of an hour learning the same rhyme. Who spent more time learning that rhyme?

   Answer ____________________

2. Betsy jogged $3\frac{5}{8}$ kilometers and walked $1\frac{6}{8}$ kilometers. What is the total length she traveled?

   Answer ____________________

3. Andrew had $630. He spent $\frac{1}{7}$ of it on earphones. He then spent $\frac{1}{3}$ of the remaining money on sneakers. How much money does Andrew have left?

   A. $290
   B. $300
   C. $330
   D. $360

4. It takes two-sixths of a box of nails to build one bird house. If you wanted to build eight bird houses, how many such boxes would you need?

   Answer ____________________

5. For her birthday, Jenny got $6\frac{3}{7}$ kilograms of sweets. After four days, her family had eaten $3\frac{5}{7}$ kilograms of the candy. How many kilograms of sweets does she have left?

   A. $3\frac{2}{7}$
   B. $2\frac{5}{7}$
   C. $2\frac{2}{7}$
   D. $1\frac{6}{7}$

6. Jessica has 4 bags of birdseed. She wants to place the birdseed into 6 bird feeders equally. How much of the bags will go in each feeder?

   Answer ____________________

7. An empty truck weighed $6\frac{4}{10}$ tons. The load weighed $4\frac{8}{10}$ tons. What would be the combined weight of the truck and the load?

   Answer ____________________

8. A cafe used seven pounds of flour during the day. If they used one-sixth as much bacon, how many pounds of bacon did they use?

   Answer ____________________

9. Mrs. Frederick purchased some apples. She used $\frac{2}{3}$ of them to make some pies. She used $\frac{1}{3}$ of the remaining apples to make some juice. She had 12 apples left. How many apples did Mrs. Frederick purchase?

   A. 54
   B. 58
   C. 62
   D. 66

10. Julia had $5\frac{3}{9}$ kilograms of pears. If she later used $3\frac{2}{6}$ kilograms in a recipe for pie, how many kilograms of pears did she have left?

    Answer ____________________

11. Wendy bought eleven packages of lollipops at the store and ate one-fourth of a package each day. How much would she have eaten after fourteen days?

    A. $2\frac{3}{4}$
    B. $3\frac{1}{4}$
    C. $4\frac{3}{4}$
    D. $3\frac{2}{4}$

12. Megan's class recycled $4\frac{3}{5}$ boxes of paper in three months. If they recycled another $9\frac{4}{5}$ boxes in the next six months, what was the total amount they recycled?

    Answer ____________________

13. There are twenty-one students in a Spanish class. $\frac{3}{7}$ of the students are girls. How many boys are in the class?

    Answer ____________________

14. Grace spent $\frac{1}{12}$ of her money on a burger. The burger costs $6. How much money did Grace have left?

    Answer ____________________

15. A bottle could hold one-third of a liter of juice. If Melany filled up fifteen bottles, how many liters of juice would she have?

    Answer ____________________

FITNESS

Please be aware of your environment and be safe at all times. If you cannot do an exercise, just try your best.

Today you get to decide which exercises you would like to do! Think of the previous exercises and select which fitness activity you would like to do.

Patterns and rules

1. The number pattern is "add 7". Which number is after 36, 43, 50, 57?

   A. 63
   B. 64
   C. 65
   D. 66

2. Which rule describes the pattern 3, 12, 48?

   A. +9
   B. +36
   C. x3
   D. x4

3. The number pattern is "subtract 11". Which number is the next 87, 76, 65, 54, ...?

   A. 45
   B. 44
   C. 43
   D. 42

4. Find the rule for the following numbers: 14, 26, 38, 50, ...

   A. Add 12
   B. Add 14
   C. Times 12
   D. Times 14

5. Find the missing numbers in this pattern 2, ___ , 8, 16, ___ , 64.

   A. 3, 24
   B. 4, 32
   C. 5, 48
   D. 6, 54

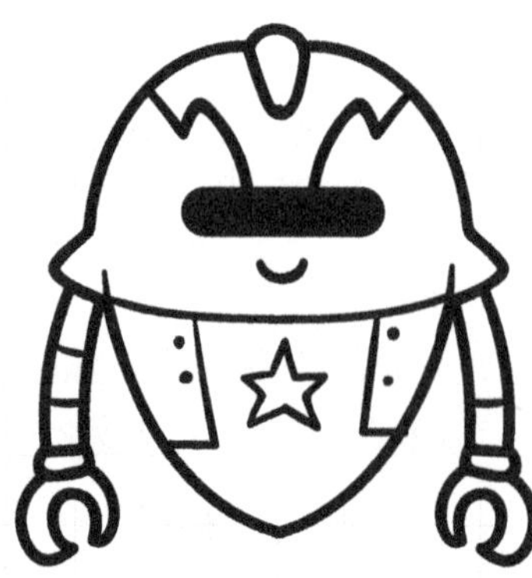

6. Which rule describes the pattern 168, 145, 122, 99, ...?

   A. - 16
   B. - 19
   C. - 23
   D. - 27

7. Determine which numbers best complete the pattern below.

   23, 35, 47, 59, ..., ...

   A. 68, 79
   B. 71, 82
   C. 71, 83
   D. 72, 85

8. The number pattern is "times 4". Which number is after 3, 12, 48, 192?

   A. 568
   B. 698
   C. 768
   D. 828

9. Which rule is used for the pattern 27, 54, 108, ...?

   A. Add 27
   B. Add 54
   C. Times 27
   D. Times 2

10. If the rule is "subtract 18", which of these numbers could be in the pattern 275, 257, 239, ...?

   A. 149
   B. 148
   C. 147
   D. 146

WEEK 7 DAY 5 MATH

11. The rule for the pattern shown below is "+ 14". Fill in the missing numbers.

    133, 147, ___ , 175,___ , 203

    Answer ____________________

12. The rule for the pattern shown is " x 5". Fill in the missing numbers.

    7, 35,___ , 875,___ , 21,875

    Answer ____________________

13. What rule is used in the number pattern 982, 936, 890, 844, ...?

    Answer ____________________

14. Start at 28 and create a pattern with the rule "add 23". What is the eighth number in the pattern?

    Answer ____________________

15. The rule for the pattern shown below is "- 17". Fill in the missing numbers.

    235,___ ,___ , 184,___ , 150

    Answer ____________________

16. Determine what rule the pattern 8, 24, 72, 216, ... is using.

    Answer ____________________

17. Start at 314 and create a pattern with the rule 'subtract 16'. What is the seventh number in the pattern?

    Answer ____________________

18. Which rule describes the pattern 32, 56, 80, 104?

    Answer ____________________

19. The rule for the pattern shown is "times 6". Fill in the missing numbers.

    9,___ , 324,___ , 11,664

    Answer ____________________

20. Determine what rule the pattern 538, 506, 474, 442, 410, ... is using.

    Answer ____________________

YOGA

Please be aware of your environment and be safe at all times. If you cannot do an exercise, just try your best.

1 - Tree Pose: Stay as long as possible.
Note: do on one leg then on another.

2 - Down Dog: 20 sec.

3 - Shavasana: 15 min.
Note: this pose is very important and provides you with long term benefits. Try not to skip this. Close your eyes and imagine who you want to be and what your goals are! Always think happy thoughts.

WEEK 7 DAY 6  EXPERIMENT

Observing Water's States of Matter: Freezing

We already know that everything is made of **matter**, but not all matter looks the same! There are three different **phases** or states of matter that we can observe in our daily lives: **liquids, solids, and gasses**. Every compound or element will exist as either a liquid (like **water**), a solid (like **iron**), or a gas (like **methane**) at room temperature. However, compounds can be changed to different phases of matter through some simple science involving temperature.

Since water is such a common (and free!) compound, we'll be using it to observe the different states of matter. First, we'll observe water in its normal, liquid state. Then, we'll transform it into a solid!

Materials:

- A freezer
- A refrigerator/freezer thermometer
- A drinking glass
- A plastic or rubber ice cube tray
- Room temperature running water
- A timer or stopwatch
- Notepaper

Procedure:

1. Place your refrigerator/freezer thermometer in the freezer and give it at least 15 minutes to adjust to the temperature. On your notepaper, make note of your freezer's temperature.
2. Pour yourself a glass of water and observe the water closely. Think of what words you could use to describe the way the water looks, smells, tastes, moves, etc. and write a short description of the liquid water on your notepaper.
3. Fill the plastic or rubber ice cube tray.
4. Place the drinking glass (at least half full) and the ice cube tray in the freezer, shut the door, and start your timer.
5. Every ten minutes, check in on your water to observe if and how it has changed. Take a few notes on your paper each time you check, noting how the appearance of the ice, the glass, and the tray have changed (if at all).
6. When you see solid ice beginning to form, look carefully at your glass or ice cube tray to determine if the ice is entirely formed, or if there is only a thin layer of ice. You can also gently poke the ice with your finger to gauge how solid it is.

WEEK 7 DAY 6  EXPERIMENT

7. When the ice cubes in the tray are fully frozen, remove the tray from the freezer and extract the ice cubes from it. Observe the solid water (ice) closely, like you did the liquid water back in Step 2, and make note of the ice's **properties.**

8. Once the glass of water is fully frozen, make note of the time in your notes, and carefully place the glass back in a sink to allow the ice to thaw. Take note of how long it takes the frozen (solid) water to melt back into its original liquid state.

Follow-Up Questions:

1. What was the difference in time between when the ice cubes froze and the glass of water froze? Why do you think that happened?

____

____

____

2. How would life be more challenging if water existed as a solid or gas at room temperature instead of a liquid?

____

____

____

YOGA

Please be aware of your environment and be safe at all times. If you cannot do an exercise, just try your best.

2 - Child Pose: 20 sec.

4 -Book Pose: 20 sec. Note: Keep your core tight. Legs shoud be across your eyes.

1 - Bend Down: 20 sec.

START

5 - Shavasana: as long as you can. Note: think of happy moments and relax your mind.

3 - Chair: 20 sec.

WEEK 7 DAY 7  MAZE

Task: What color is the scarf? Paint it!

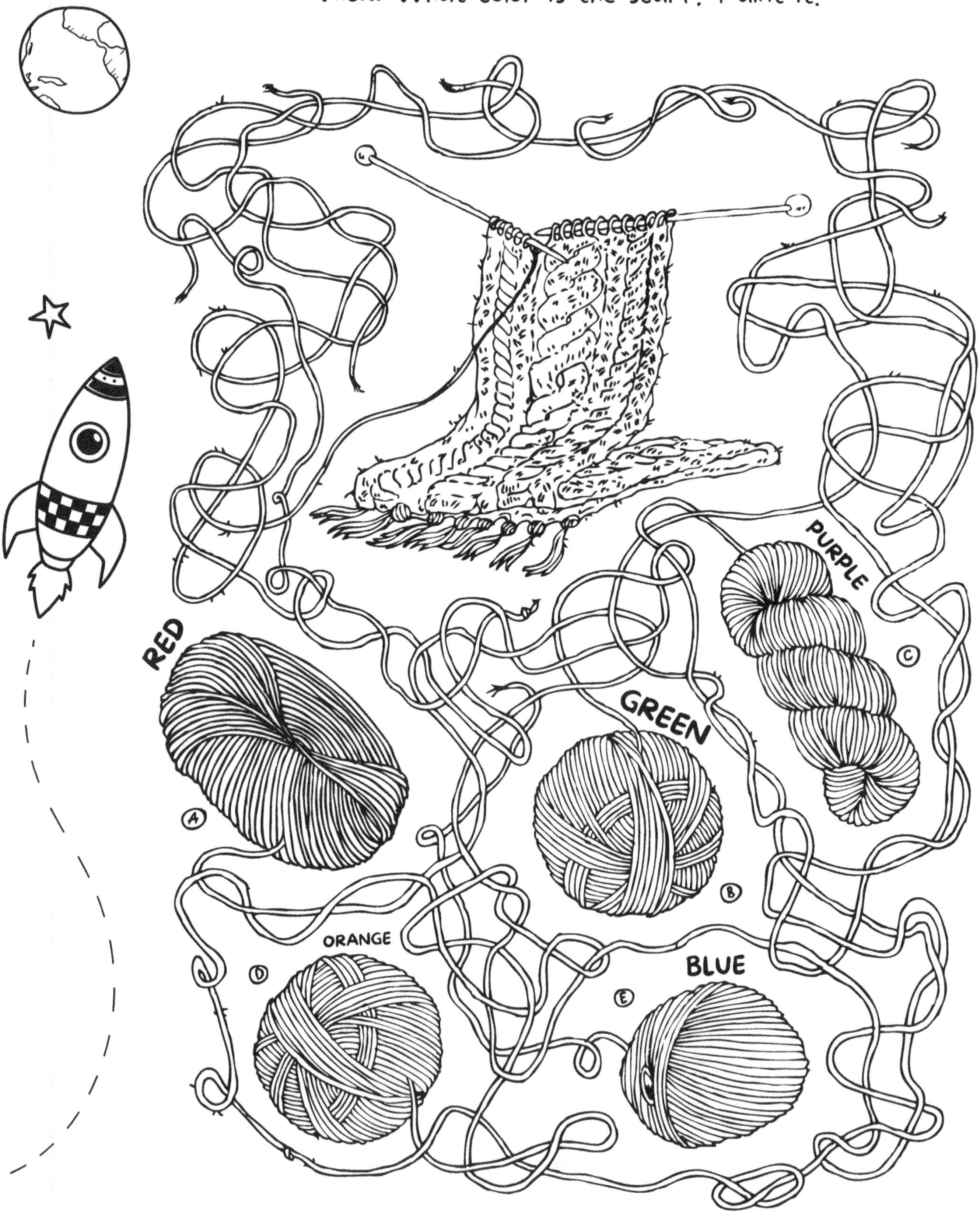

RED

Ⓐ

PURPLE

Ⓒ

GREEN

Ⓑ

ORANGE

Ⓓ

BLUE

Ⓔ

Answer: ___________________________

Are you freezing?
Last week we were on planet Uranus, which we learned was super cold. Are you ready to travel to Neptune?
WEEK 8
Neptune has a very active climate.
In 1989, the Great Dark Spot was a massive storm on Neptune that lasted about five years. According to data, wind speeds reached up to 1,500 miles per hour. That's scary!

WEEK 8 DAY 1

OVERVIEW OF ENGLISH CONCEPTS

IDENTIFYING EVIDENCE & SUPPORT IN NONFICTION TEXTS

Now that you're a professional at determining main ideas, it's time to dig a little deeper and start to think about how authors make their points and demonstrate their thinking to the reader. In nonfiction texts, authors use **evidence** (proof) to show why their perspective is accurate and provide **support** (examples and explanations) to make things as clear and easy to understand for the reader as possible.

In order to determine how good a job a writer is doing at making their point, you need to be ready to identify and assess their support. As you read, ask yourself, "Do I think this author is doing a good job explaining this? What strategies and information are they using to clarify their point or perspective?"

Here are a few key strategies to help you transform into an evidence-and-support finding machine!

Key Strategies:

- Always start by **determining the main idea first!**
  - If you have questions about how to do that, review Week 7!
  - If you haven't identified the main idea, you can't possibly know what the author is supporting, so it's pointless to start by looking for support!
- Look for any **vocabulary** or **terms** the author defines for the reader
  - The author may be trying to clarify his or her perspective by teaching the reader technical language that helps them see things from a more specific point of view
- Pull out **examples** the author uses
  - Are the examples easy to understand and clearly connected to the main idea?
    - If so, they are probably strong support
    - If not, the author is probably doing a poor job supporting their point
- Look at how the author **connects ideas**
  - Well-supported writing has a clear flow, meaning one idea or aspect of the topic will naturally lead into the next idea or aspect
  - If the author's thinking and writing are clear, you should be able to see the connections between all the different ideas and follow the flow of the piece

REMEMBER, the author is including evidence and support for you - the reader. That means they should be including the most valuable, easy-to-understand information to help you build a deep knowledge of the topic and understanding of their viewpoint. When you write, you need to do the same for your readers!

From "Renaissance and Reformation"

By John Lord

It was while Galileo was a student in the university of his native city that his attention was arrested by the vibrations of a lamp suspended from the ceiling of the cathedral; and before he had quitted the church, while the choir was chanting medieval anthems, he had compared those vibrations with his own pulse, which after repeated experiments, ended in the construction of the first pendulum, - applied not as it was by Huygens to the measurement of time, but to medical science, to enable physicians to ascertain the rate of the pulse...

Galileo had been destined by his father to the profession of medicine, and was ignorant of mathematics. He amused his leisure hours with painting and music, and in order to study the principles of drawing he found it necessary to acquire some knowledge of geometry, much to the annoyance of his father, who did not like to see his mind diverted from the prescriptions of Hippocrates and Galen. The certain truths of geometry burst upon him like a revelation, and after mastering Euclid he turned to Archimedes with equal enthusiasm. Mathematics now absorbed his mind, and the father was obliged to yield to the bent of his genius, which seemed to disdain the regular professions by which social position was most surely effected.

He wrote about this time in an essay on the Hydrostatic Balance, which introduced him to Guido Ubaldo, a famous mathematician, who induced him to investigate the subject of the centre of gravity in solid bodies. His treatise on this subject secured an introduction to the Grand Duke of Tuscany, who perceived his merits, and by whom he was appointed a lecturer on mathematics at Pisa, but on the small salary of sixty crowns a year.

1. What does the first paragraph reveal about Galileo's personality or character?

2. According to the passage, how did Galileo get interested in math?

3. Which of these best describes the main ideas of Paragraph 2?

   A. Galileo's father recognized his talent for math early and wanted him to be a mathematician.
   B. Galileo's father always wanted his son to be a doctor and did not accept that Galileo wanted to be a scientist and mathematician.
   C. Galileo's father wanted his son to be a mathematician, but when he saw the pulse-measuring pendulum he created, he decided that Galileo should be a doctor.
   D. Galileo's father always wanted his son to be a doctor, but when he saw his ability in math, he ultimately allowed Galileo to follow his talent and passion.

4. Based on context clues, who were Hippocrates and Galen?

   A. Famous scientists
   B. Famous artists
   C. Famous doctors
   D. Famous mathematicians

5. In your own words, what are the **main ideas** of this passage?

Brainstorming Support for Main Ideas

Directions:

Read each main idea and brainstorm three different sentences that could be used to support, describe, or clarify that main idea. Write your sentences on the lines below:

1. **MAIN IDEA:** Teachers should assign less homework.

(A) ______________________________

____

(B) ______________________________

____

(C) ______________________________

____

2. **MAIN IDEA:** It's important to dispose of trash correctly and not to litter.

(A) ______________________________

____

(B) ______________________________

____

(C) ______________________________

____

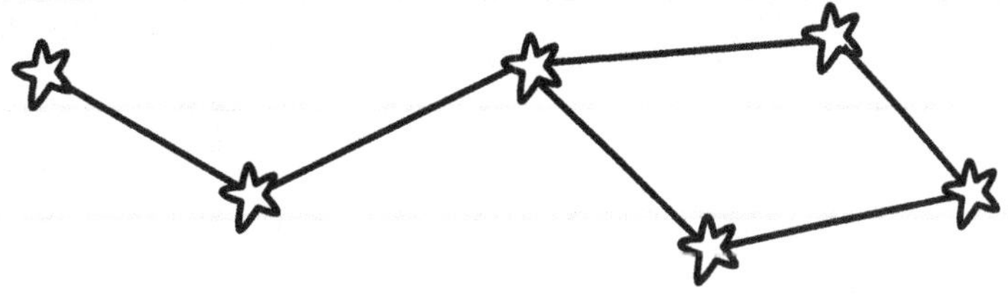

3. **MAIN IDEA:** ____________________ is the best school subject. (Fill in the blank with the topic or class of your choice before brainstorming your support sentences.)

(A) ____

____

(B) ____

____

(C) ____

____

FITNESS

Please be aware of your environment and be safe at all times. If you cannot do an exercise, just try your best.

Repeat these exercises **3 ROUNDS**

3 - Plank: 15 sec.

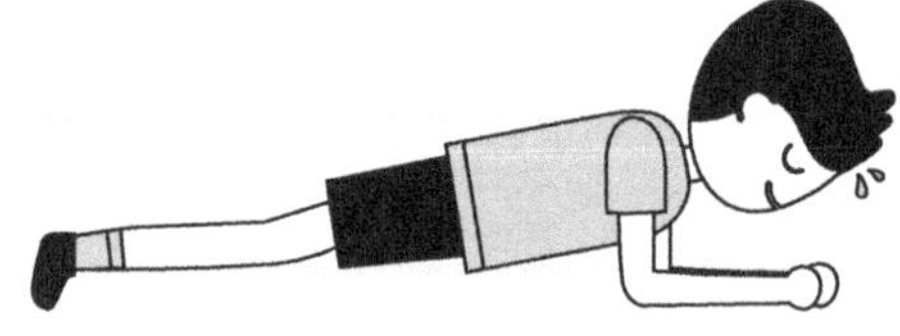

2 - Abs: 10 times

4 - Run: 50m
Note: Run **25** meters to one side and **25** meters back to the starting position.

1 - Bend forward: 10 times.
Note: try to touch your feet. Make sure to keep your back straight and if needed you can bend your knees.

From "The Story of Manhattan"

By Charles Hemstreet

The long and narrow Island of Manhattan was a wild and beautiful spot in the year 1609. In this year a little ship sailed up the bay below the island, took the river to the west, and went on. In these days there were no tall houses with white walls glistening in the sunlight, no church-spires, no noisy hum of running trains, no smoke to blot out the blue sky. None of these things. But in their place were beautiful trees with spreading branches, stretches of sand-hills, and green patches of grass. In the branches of the trees there were birds of varied colors, and wandering through the tangled undergrowth were many wild animals. The people of the island were men and women who were natives; strong and healthy people who clothed themselves in the furs of animals and made their houses of the trees and vines.

In this year of 1609, these people gathered on the shore of their island and looked with wonder at the boat, so different from any they had ever seen, as it was swept before the wind up the river.

The ship was called the Half Moon, and it had come all the way from Amsterdam, in the Dutch Netherlands. The Netherlands was quite a small country in the northern part of Europe, not nearly as large as the State of New York, and was usually called Holland, as Holland was the most important of its several states. But the Dutch owned other lands than these. They had islands in the Indian Ocean that were rich in spices of every sort, and the other European countries needed these spices. These islands, being quite close to India, were called the East Indies, and the company of Dutch merchants who did most of the business with them was called the East India Company. They had many ships, and the Half Moon was one of them.

It was a long way to the East India Islands from Holland, for in these days there was no Suez Canal to separate Asia and Africa, and the ships had to go around Africa by way of the Cape of Good Hope. Besides being a long distance, it was a dangerous passage; for although from its name one might take the Cape of Good Hope to be a very pleasant place, the winds blew there with great force, and the waves rolled so high that they often dashed the fragile ships to pieces.

1. Based on the passage, what did Manhattan look like when the Dutch first arrived there?

2. Based on the passage, what was the role of spices in the discovery of Manhattan?

3. Which detail could be added to Paragraph 4 to help the reader understand the connection between the Cape of Good Hope and Manhattan?

   A. An explanation that Dutch sailors were trying to sail through North America to avoid going around the Cape of Good Hope.
   B. A more specific description of the weather near the Cape of Good Hope.
   C. A description of the weather near Manhattan, to contrast with the Cape of Good Hope.
   D. A description of the difference in miles between going around the Cape of Good Hope and sailing to Manhattan.

4. Based on Paragraphs 3 and 4, where were the crew of the Half Moon hoping to arrive?

   A. Manhattan
   B. Holland
   C. The Cape of Good Hope
   D. The islands of the West Indies

5. What details or ideas does the author introduce to prove that the Dutch were very important during the time in history described throughout the passage?

Brainstorming Support for Main Ideas

Part 2

Directions:

Read each main idea and brainstorm three different sentences that could be used to support, describe, or clarify that main idea. Write your sentences on the lines below:

1. **MAIN IDEA:** Summer is the best time of the year.

(A) ____

____

(B) ____

____

(C) ____

____

2. **MAIN IDEA:** Refrigerators are extremely important to our current way of life.

(A) ____

____

(B) ____

____

(C) ____

____

ACTIVITIES

IDENTIFYING EVIDENCE & SUPPORT IN NONFICTION TEXTS

3. **MAIN IDEA:** ____________________ is the best movie I've ever seen. (Fill in the blank with the topic or class of your choice before brainstorming your support sentences.)

(A) ____

____

(B) ____

____

(C) ____

____

FITNESS

Please be aware of your environment and be safe at all times. If you cannot do an exercise, just try your best.

Repeat these exercises **3 ROUNDS**

1 - Squats: 15 times. Note: imagine you are trying to sit on a chair.

2 - Side Bending: 10 times to each side. Note: try to touch your feet.

3 - Tree Pose: Stay as long as possible. Note: do the same with the other leg.

4 - High Plank: 15 sec.

5 - Abs: 10 times

Money

1. How much money is shown below?

Answer ____________________

2. Determine the amount of money shown below.

A. $67
B. $72
C. $74
D. $79

3. How much money is shown below?

A. $37 and 32¢
B. $42 and 52¢
C. $47 and 67¢
D. $49 and 32¢

4. What is 4 pennies represented as a decimal of $1?

A. 0.40
B. 0.04
C. 1.4
D. 1.04

5. Write the amount of the coins below as a decimal of $1.

Answer ____________________

6. If 12 dollars and 37 cents is subtracted from 25 dollars and 28 cents, what do we get?

A. 11 dollars and 29 cents
B. 12 dollars and 31 cents
C. 12 dollars and 71 cents
D. 12 dollars and 91 cents

7. What is $36.42 added to $45.68?

A. $79.20
B. $82.10
C. $82.60
D. $83.50

8. Complete the addition statement:
$56 and 87¢ + $___ and ___¢ = $63 and 14¢.

Answer ____________________

9. Two years ago, Mr. Jackman spent three hundred ninety-one thousand, seven hundred and fifty dollars on buying a new house. How would you write the cost of the new house in digits?

Answer ____________________

10. Jonathan had **$30.00**. He bought two pairs of gloves each for **$7.65** and four pairs of socks each for **$1.75**. How much money did he have left?

Answer ____________________

Angles

1. Tick the boxes that could be applied to each angle.

Angle	Acute	Obtuse	Right
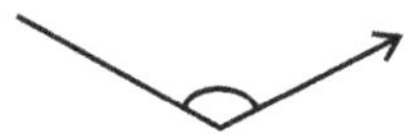			

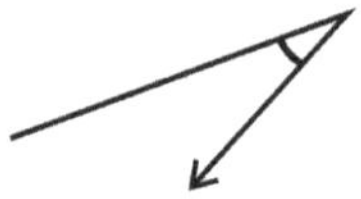			

2. What type of marked angle does this shape have?

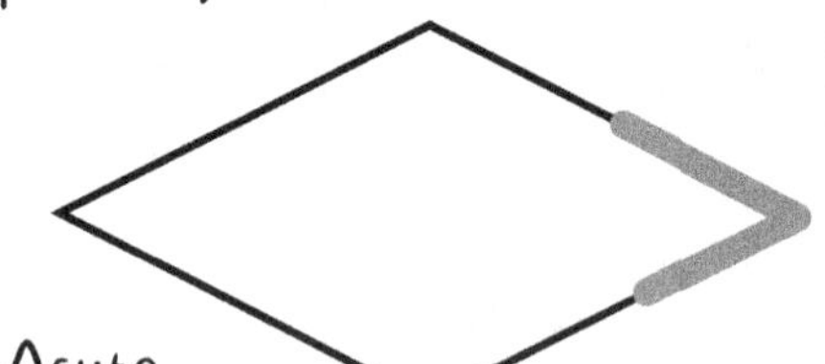

A. Acute
B. Obtuse
C. Right
D. None of the above

FITNESS

 Please be aware of your environment and be safe at all times. If you cannot do an exercise, just try your best.

Repeat these exercises
3 ROUNDS

1 - Bend forward: 10 times.
Note: try to touch your feet. Make sure to keep your back straight and if needed you can bend your knees.

2 - Lunges: 5 times to each leg.
Note: Use your body weight or books as weight to do leg lunges.

3 - Plank: 15 sec.

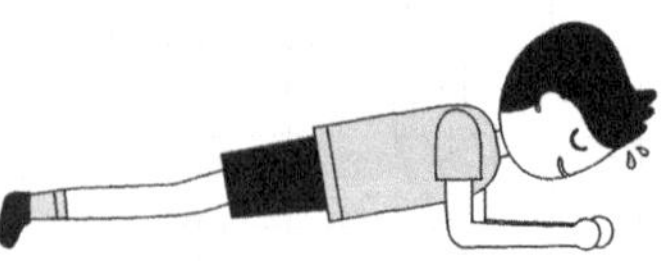

4 - Abs: 10 times

Angles

1. Is this angle less than, equal to, or greater than a right angle?

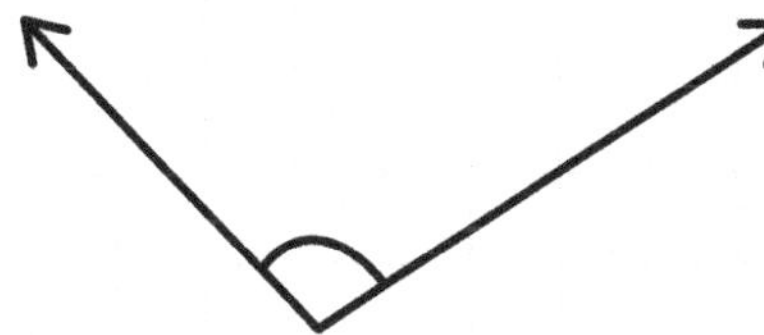

Answer ____________________

2. For the shape below, count the number of angles of each type.

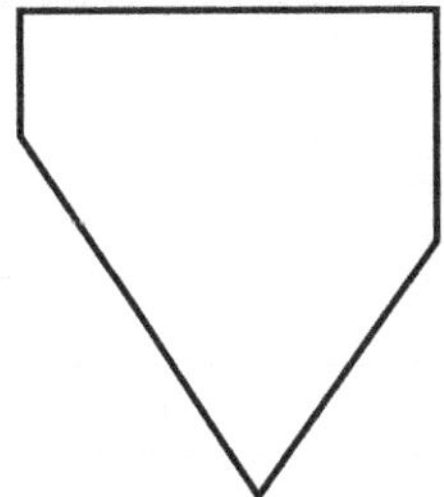

Number of acute angles _______

Number of obtuse angles _______

Number of right angles _______

3. Identify each angle of the shape below. (Acute, Obtuse or Right)

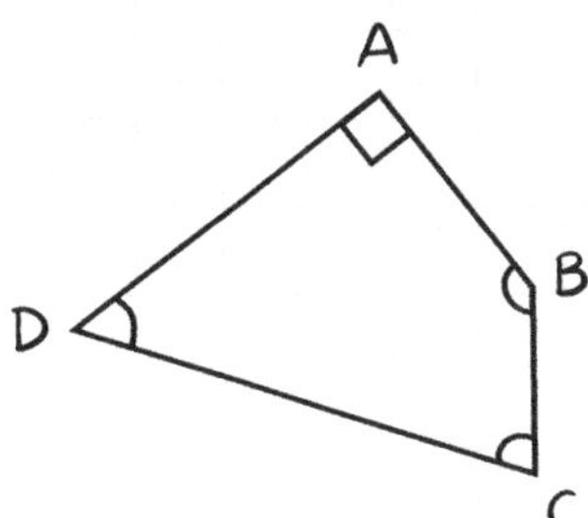

A. ___________

B. ___________

C. ___________

D. ___________

4. Tick the boxes that could be applied to each angle.

Angle	Acute	Obtuse	Right
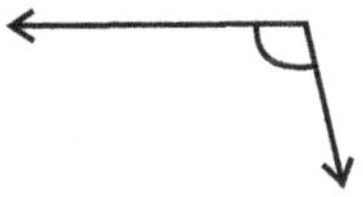			

5. Is this angle less than, equal to, or greater than a right angle?

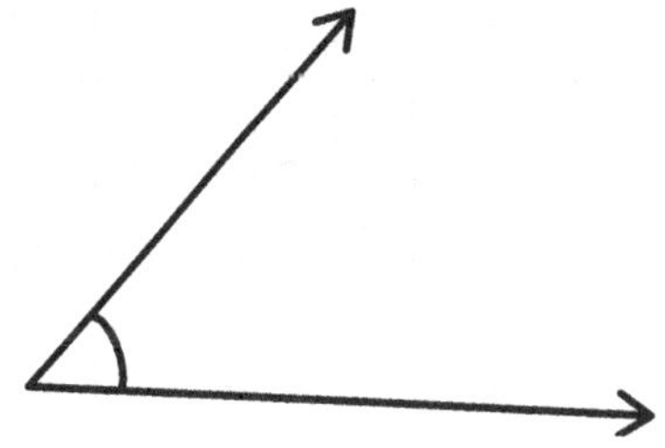

Answer ____________________

6. What is the measurement of this angle? Choose the best estimate.

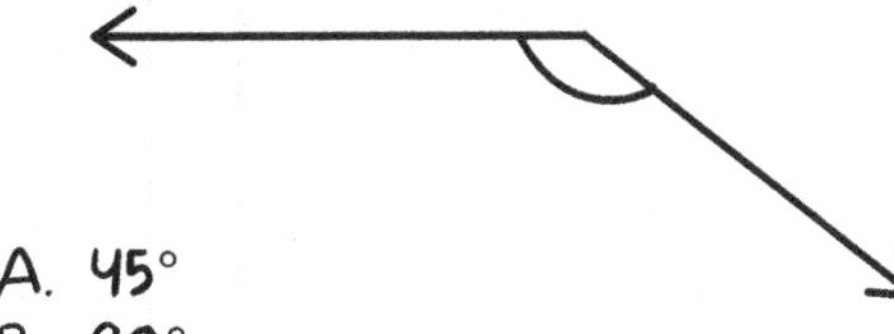

A. 45°
B. 90°
C. 135°
D. 170°

MATH

7. Classify each angle as acute, obtuse or right.

   A. 30° ________________
   B. 90° ________________
   C. 100° ________________
   D. 75° ________________

8. For the shape below, count the number of angles of each type.

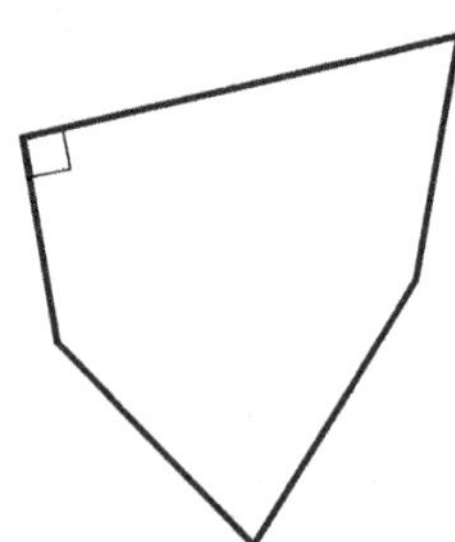

Number of acute angles _______
Number of obtuse angles _______
Number of right angles _______

Triangles, Squares, Rectangles

1. What kind of triangle is this?

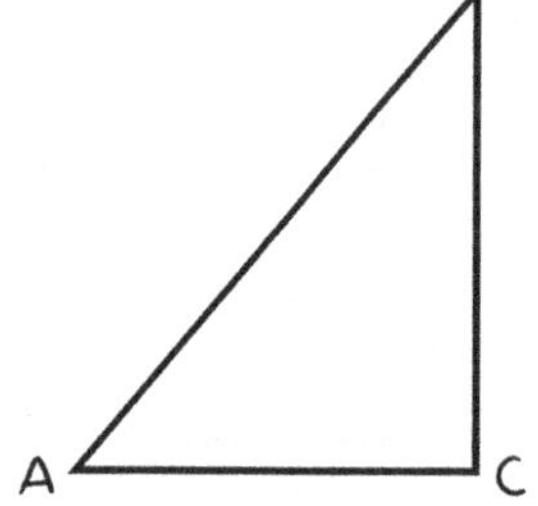

   A. Acute
   B. Obtuse
   C. Right
   D. Equilateral

2. If a quadrilateral has all angles that measure 90° and the length and width is not the same measurement, what kind of quadrilateral is it?

   Answer ____________________

3. A triangle has the angle measurements of 95°, 45° and 40°. What kind of triangle is it?

   A. Equilateral triangle
   B. Scalene triangle
   C. Isosceles triangle
   D. Right triangle

FITNESS

Please be aware of your environment and be safe at all times. If you cannot do an exercise, just try your best.

Repeat these exercises **3 ROUNDS**

1 - High Plank: 15 sec.

2 - Abs: 10 times

3 - Side Bending: 10 times to each side. Note: try to touch your feet.

Triangles, Squares, Rectangles

1. A triangle has side lengths of 8 centimeters, 7 centimeters and 9 centimeters. What kind of triangle is it?

Answer ____________________

Using the shapes below, answer questions 2 -3.

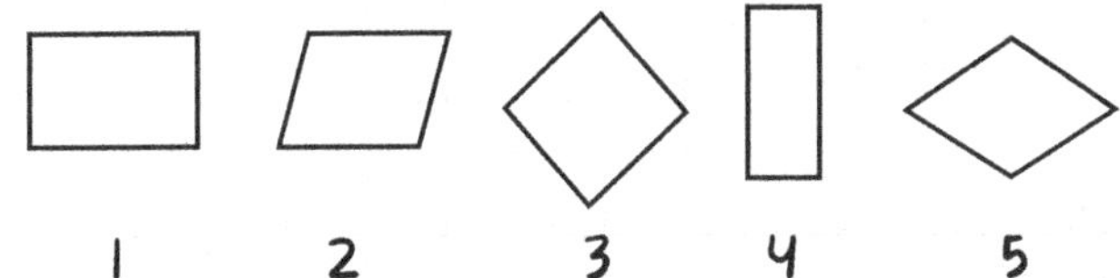

2. Which shapes are rectangles?

A. 1, 3, 4
B. 1, 2, 4
C. 3, 4
D. 1, 3, 5

3. Which shape is a square?

A. 1
B. 2
C. 3
D. 4

4. A triangle has the angle measurements of 32°, 90° and 58°. What kind of triangle is it?

Answer ____________________

5. What kind of triangle is this?

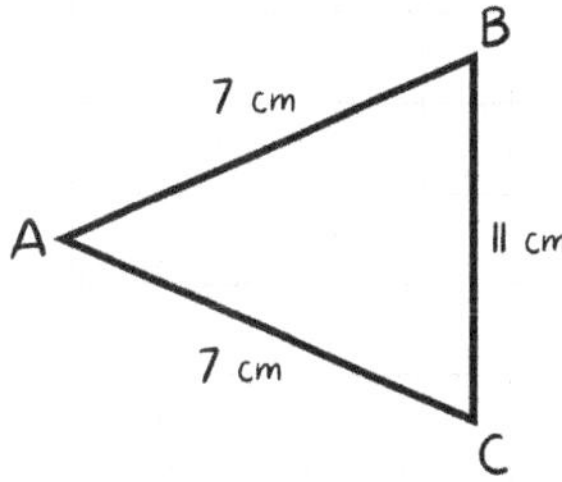

A. Equilateral
B. Scalene
C. Isosceles
D. Right

6. If a rectangle has all sides that are equal, it is also called a ____.

Answer ____________________

7. A quadrilateral has angles of 90° and sides of 12 cm, 4 cm, 12 cm, 4 cm . What kind of quadrilateral is it?

Answer ____________________

Circles

Use the drawing below to answer questions 1 - 2.

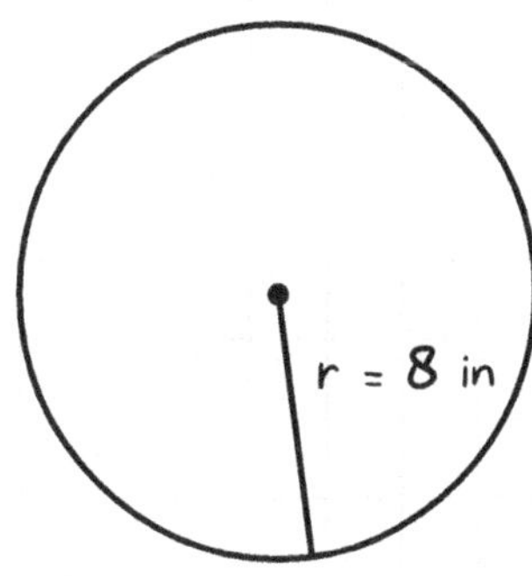

1. What is the diameter of the circle?

Answer ____________________

2. What is the circumference of the circle? Use π as 3. Note: circumference formula is $2\pi r$.

Answer ____________________

WEEK 8 DAY 5  MATH

Use the drawing below to answer questions 3 - 7. Point O is the center of the circle.

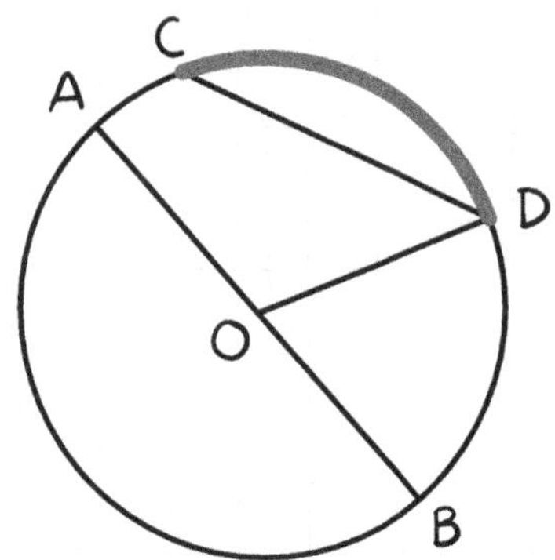

3. What is AB? Is this a diameter, radius, or a chord? Explain how you know.

   Answer ______________________

4. What is OD? Is this a diameter, radius, or a chord? Explain how you know.

   Answer ______________________

5. A chord is a straight line segment that has both endpoints that lie on a circle. The diameter is actually a chord. Can you find another chord that is shown on the circle? What is this chord?

   Answer ______________________

6. Explain the difference between a radius and diameter.

   Answer ______________________

7. What is point O?

   Answer ______________________

8. The radius of a circle is 27 feet. What is its diameter?

   Answer ______________________

9. The radius of a circle is 14 cm. What is its circumference? Use π as 3. Note: circumference formula is $2\pi r$.

   Answer ______________________

10. The circumference is 216 yards. What is the diameter of a circle? Use π as 3. Note: circumference formula is $2\pi r$.

    Answer ______________________

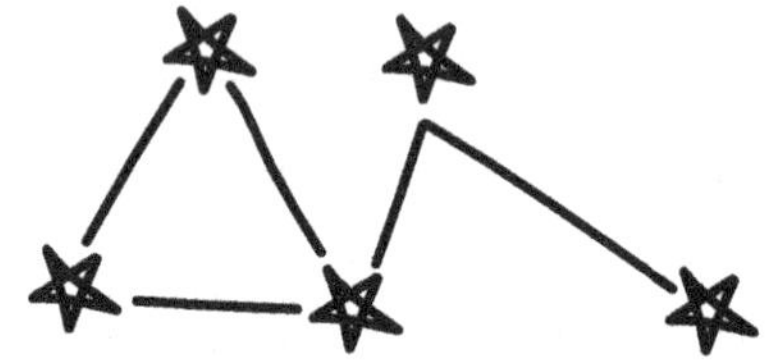

YOGA ☆

Please be aware of your environment and be safe at all times. If you cannot do an exercise, just try your best.

1 - Tree Pose: Stay as long as possible.
Note: do on one leg then on another.

2 - Down Dog: 20 sec.

3 - Shavasana: 15 min.
Note: this pose is very important and provides you with long term benefits. Try not to skip this. Close your eyes and imagine who you want to be and what your goals are! Always think happy thoughts.

WEEK 8 DAY 6  EXPERIMENT

Observing Water's States of Matter: Evaporation

Last week, we saw that a liquid can be turned into a solid through a process known as **freezing**. Now, we'll look at how we can turn a liquid into a **gas**. We call this process **evaporation**! Today, we'll be doing two different, but connected, investigations with water to explore the concept of evaporation.

Materials:

- Room temperature running water
- Measuring cups or spoons
- Two identical bowls (nothing fancy - they'll be going outside)
- A stovetop or hotplate
- A small cookpot
- An adult (for supervision)
- A watch or timer
- Notepaper

Procedure:

1. Using your measuring cups or spoons, place two cups of water in each of the two bowls and the small cookpot.
2. Place the two bowls outside, one in a shady place (like a covered porch, under a tree, etc.) and one in the sunniest possible spot you can find nearby. Make note of the time when you started. (**Note:** It's important to do this experiment on a reasonably sunny day. If the weather doesn't allow for this activity, you can do the Week 9 experiment instead.)
3. With some help from an adult, put the small cookpot on a stovetop burner and turn the heat up to high. Start your timer.
4. Stay close by with your parent and observe the pot as the water begins to boil. What do you see and hear as the water gets hot? Write your observations in your notes and be sure to include how long it took the water to reach a boil.
5. As the water boils, observe the steam that rises up out of the pot. You will also notice that the water level in the pot is gradually shrinking - that's because heat is turning the liquid water into a gas (which we call steam). (**Note:** This steam can be extremely hot, so it's important not to touch it.)
6. When the water level in the pot gets low, be sure to turn off the burner. It's important not to let the water evaporate completely, as that could lead to the pot being damaged.
7. Wait a few hours until it's close to sunset, and retrieve your bowls from the outside, being careful not to spill any of the water that remains in them.
8. Using your measuring cups or spoons, measure how much water is left in each of the bowls. Write the totals down in your notes and compare the amount of water missing from the sunny bowl to the amount from the shady bowl.

WEEK 8 DAY 6  EXPERIMENT

Follow-Up Questions:

1. How was what happened to the outdoor bowls similar to what happened in the cookpot on the stove? What force or object was acting like the burner?

____

____

____

2. Based on what you saw, why do you think boiling water is often used for cooking food?

____

____

____

____

____

YOGA

Please be aware of your environment and be safe at all times. If you cannot do an exercise, just try your best.

2 - Child Pose: 20 sec.

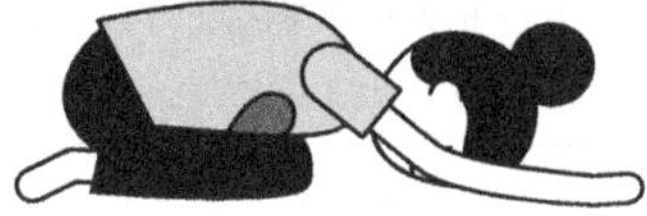

4 -Book Pose: 20 sec. Note: Keep your core tight. Legs shoud be across your eyes.

1 - Bend Down: 20 sec.

5 - Shavasana: as long as you can. Note: think of happy moments and relax your mind.

START

3 - Chair: 20 sec.

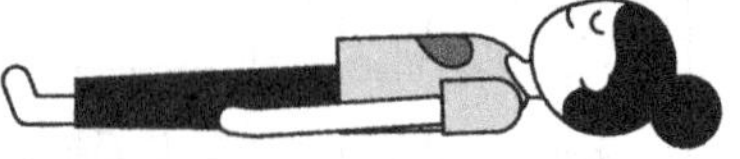

WEEK 8 DAY 7  MAZE

Task: The electric wires are all messed up. Which lamp is switched on?

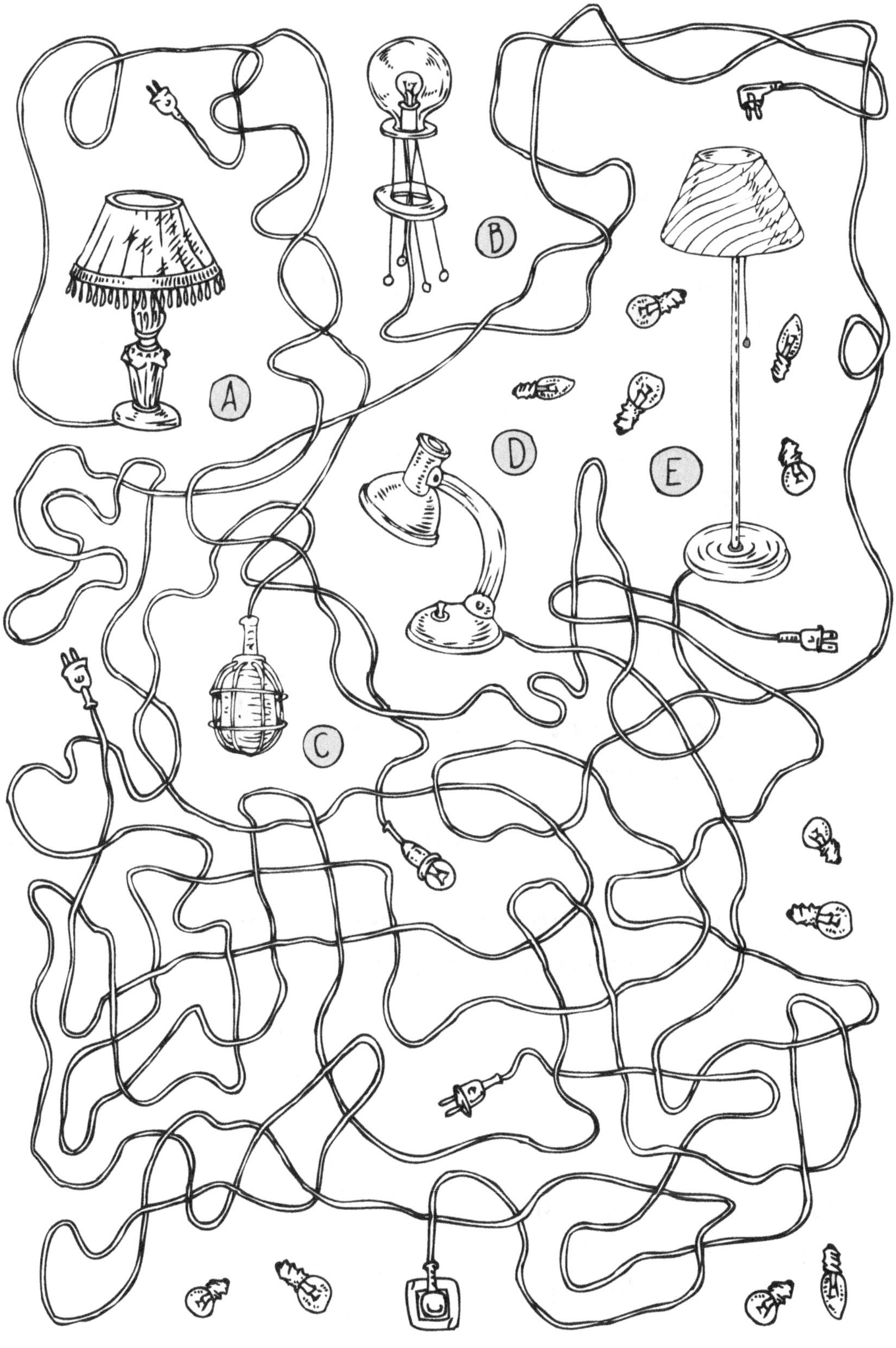

Answer: ______________________________

Answer Sheets

To see the answer key to the entire workbook, you can easily download the answer key from our website!

*Due to the high request from parents and teachers, we have removed the answer key from the workbook so you do not need to rip out the answer key while students work on the workbook.

Go to **argoprep.com/summer5**
OR scan the QR Code:

Place your mouse over the workbook you have, and you will see the "Download Answers" button.

For detailed video instructions on how to access the "Answer Sheets," please scan this QR code.

Kids Summer Academy by ArgoPrep: Grade 8-9

Kids Summer Academy by ArgoPrep: Grade 5-6

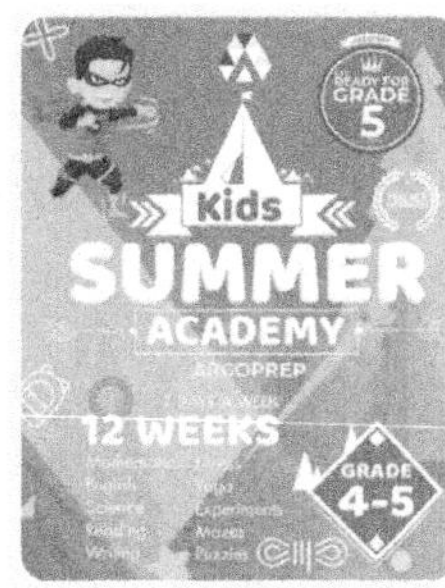

Kids Summer Academy by ArgoPrep: Grade 4-5

Kids Summer Academy by ArgoPrep: Grade 6-7

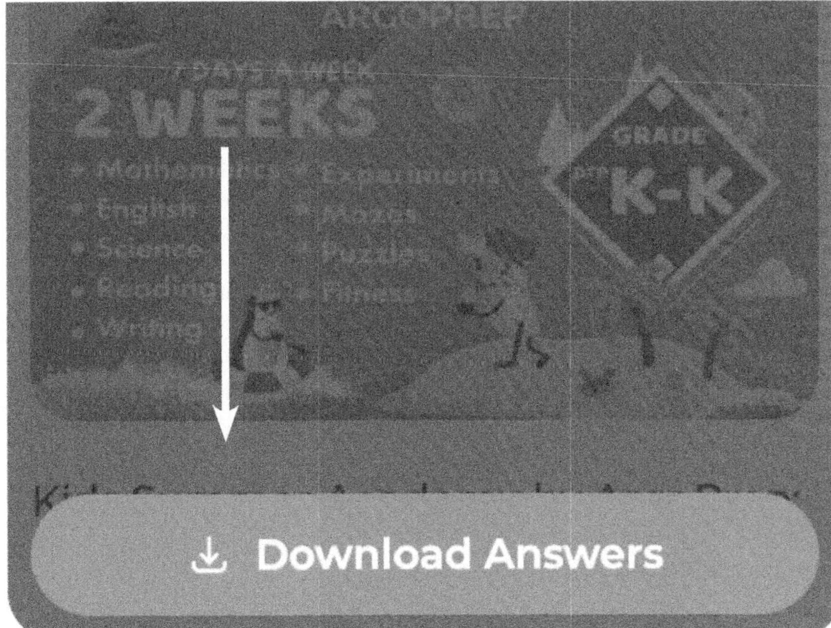

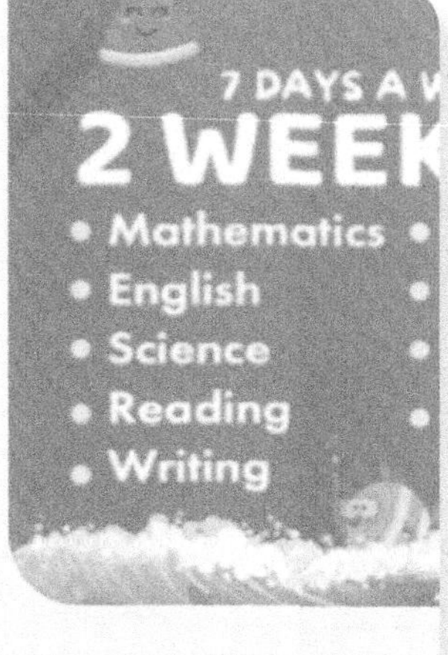

Kids Summer
Grade 8-9